TALKING DONKEYS and SMASHING BABIES

Musings of the Lesbian Daughter of
an Evangelical Minister

DR. MARA HOLLIS

authorHOUSE®

AuthorHouse™
1663 Liberty Drive
Bloomington, IN 47403
www.authorhouse.com
Phone: 1-800-839-8640

Published by AuthorHouse 7/29/2013

ISBN: 978-1-4817-2606-1 (sc)
ISBN: 978-1-4817-2605-4 (e)

Library of Congress Control Number: 2013911185

Any people depicted in stock imagery provided by Thinkstock are models, and such images are being used for illustrative purposes only. Certain stock imagery © Thinkstock.

This book is printed on acid-free paper.

TABLE OF CONTENTS

DISCOVERY

I DROPPED THAT BOOK like it was a hot potato. It is amazing how a small, seemingly innocuous, inanimate object that weighed no more than two pounds, with no sharp or jagged edges, containing no poisonous substances - nothing that would physically harm anything unless hurled with great force - could elicit such fear. I had just climbed into the back seat of my parents' Crown Victoria. (Do old ministers drive anything else?) While waiting for my parents to join me in the car, I casually leaned over to see what Mother had been reading. I assumed it was the usual, typical religious literature. The only books in our household had titles like: *The Free Will Baptist, How to be a Christian Husband, How to be an Obedient Christian Wife,* or *Jesus Teaches about Family.*

"So Your Child is Gay!" screamed the title. Oh my God! They, or at least, she, knew! Maybe it was just a suspicion. Maybe they were talking about my sister. No, she had been infatuated with boys since she was young. She went crazy when her favorite boy stars appeared on television and always swooned when talking about her boyfriends. No, it had to be me.

I can't imagine what gave me away – my undying love for flannel, my complete disinterest in boys, the sparkle in my eyes when watching the Lennon Sisters sing on TV, my utter disdain for anything

1

feminine (except other girls), my declaration at a very early age that there was no way I was getting married and having babies, or the girls I kept bringing home who were androgynous in both appearance and behavior. I thought I had successfully contained my emotions, although admittedly I always feared a discovery. Sometimes it felt as if I were on the verge of an incredible eruption of those pent-up feelings that could never be conveyed; I felt as if I would forever be confined to a secretive and isolated existence.

Realizing that something was terribly wrong compelled me to sit and ruminate about how my life had unfolded. Why had I, a liberal thinking lesbian, ended up with an evangelical minister, his obedient wife (most of the time), and their other two children as my family? They – my Dad, Mom and two sisters, would probably say that my soul was sent to this particular family so it could be saved. I choose to believe that the fateful intent was for me to free them from the bondages of prejudice. I think neither of us has succeeded. To get along, we just choose not to discuss politics or religion. My parents' mantra is, "If you don't believe as I do, you are wrong." Until a few years ago, my father believed Catholics were going to hell because they prayed to Mary (a false idol). He has since changed his mind about that but still believes firmly that all non-Christians will meet their fate with the devil. I guess I will be one of those if I don't live long enough to repent and "straighten up."

I decided to try to find out why I was so strange, so different from others. I had no idea why I was the way I was, and what made other people tick, but I was certainly interested in finding out, so I majored in psychology. I discovered almost immediately that this Nature-Nurture debate had been going on for years, and there were no definitive conclusions. Some people believe that nature (genetics) contributes more and others believe nurture (environment) is more responsible for our eventual outcomes. But, we are all products of our heredity and environment. Simple enough.

But that didn't answer the question to which I wanted a specific and conclusive response: Why am I homosexual, especially when I have been told time and time again that it is one of the most egregious sins? The idea that homosexuality was sinful was so ingrained in us, I didn't even acknowledge I was gay until I was a junior in college. My attraction to one of my dorm buddies was so strong, it was as if I had been slapped in the face with the realization that I was a lesbian. I had written papers on the subject for my psychology and sociology classes and still repressed the fact that I was one of them, even though I never felt a strong attraction to the opposite sex. I never had a desire to kiss or hug the guys I dated, and could not understand their obsession with these things. I had daydreamed about kissing girls, but knew it was taboo, and those daydreams could never be revealed to anyone. Homosexuality was something I did not want to acknowledge because homosexuals were people that were mocked and ridiculed. My older sister's favorite joke was "Did you hear about the queer who couldn't hear?" She would say it in a very low voice so the person being joked would respond, "Huh?" She would, again, say, "Did you hear about the queer who couldn't hear?" either in a very low voice or very fast to elicit the response another time or two, and then very plainly and loudly say, "Did you hear about the queer who couldn't hear?"

Homosexuality in the 70's when I came out (to myself, at least), was still off most people's radar. There were no public discussions; few private disclosures even. Most people at that time did not know anyone who was gay. There were no famous people advocating for gay rights, no politicians who supported gay rights (that would have been a death sentence), and no major films or television shows that highlighted us in any favorable ways. Most of us were terrified that

3

someone would find out because we knew it could potentially affect our friendships, employment, and housing options. So, we remained in the farthest corners of the darkest closets.

Prior to my introduction into the gay world, I had straight friends I knew and loved. I felt like a liar and a fake by hiding this very important part of myself from them. It was difficult to find liberal-minded others, and mistakes in assumptions could have dire consequences. My fears were so ingrained, I never approached anyone. But some brave souls' gaydar was activated by me, and I was soon swept off my feet by these interesting, rebellious, yet loving lesbians who introduced me to the other secret club members and dared invite me to the "bar" that catered to people like me. I had no idea there were so many other gays. I wasn't the only one in the entire world after all!

I will have to admit, it was a culture shock. I had never seen two women or men dancing together. I had seen the obligatory hug between male relatives, but never affectionate hugging or kissing. Admittedly, it took me a while to get used to it. I am not fond of public affection whether it be straights or gays indulging.

The first straight person to whom I disclosed was my college roommate, Sandra. Her acceptance line was one of the sweetest I have ever heard. "Mara," she said, "I'm so happy for you." "I knew you would understand," I countered, "But why are you happy?" "Because I was afraid you would never fall in love, and you've been trying to fall in love with men, and it just didn't work for you – because you love women!" Don't we wish everyone were that understanding?

The second straight person to whom I revealed my real self was another of my supportive college friends, whose only negative reaction stemmed from the fact that I had not told her earlier, and she had no clue that I was anything but heterosexual.

Very few people were trusted or close enough to share my intimate secrets, and I lived in fear of disclosure. After exposure to so many negative comments, accusations, and promises of spending eternity in hell, it was difficult in the South to garner a sense of pride. But as our numbers grew and we were emboldened, it became easier to proudly proclaim, "We're here, we're queer, get used to it." None of my friends did this out loud; of course, we were all still very closeted, and to some extent still are. Many of my friends choose discretion, and do not wish to push the envelope with our Bible-thumping, homophobic friends, relatives and co-workers.

It truly is remarkable, however, that just within my lifetime, we have emerged from a voiceless, faceless, powerless faction to a powerful political movement consisting of millions. We are so plentiful that virtually everyone, with the exception of those who do not associate in anything but heterogeneous groups, now knows someone who is gay. We are forever indebted to those fearless pioneers, political activists, entertainers, and politicians who forged the way to acceptance for those of us who have been marginalized because of misunderstandings, intolerance, bigotry, hatred, and religious persecution.

MAKING FUN

◇◇◇◇◇◇◇◇◇◇◇◇◇◇◇◇◇◇◇◇◇◇◇◇◇◇◇◇◇◇◇

MY FATHER, WHO WAS quite effeminate and took every advantage of Halloween to dress like a woman, was quick to make fun of other effeminate men. The only guy I enjoyed dating in high school was Ricky, who, as you may assume, was also gay. Neither of us knew that at the time, but Dad took great pleasure in calling him "Sicky Ricky" in an effeminate voice. When Ricky and I finally found out each other was gay, he told me all the women he dated in high school turned out to be gay. He jokingly asked if it was something he had done, or hadn't done. I guess we are just pretty good at finding each other, even if we don't really even know ourselves.

My father just seems to enjoy making fun of other people and calling attention to their imperfections. He is notorious for announcing "Look at how fat that woman is," when an overweight woman would appear, or "That is the ugliest woman I have ever seen," when a less than attractive women emerged. My sisters and I have begged and pleaded with him, and explained how dangerous this behavior is, to no avail. Because of his loud voice, we explained that he runs the risk of getting into a serious verbal or physical altercation by either the subject of his denigrations or one of his or her loved ones. I think he really believes that since he is so old he is safe now – for who would hit an old man? - and seems to delight in making his opinions known to everyone around him.

To this minister father of mine, church members were not immune. I cannot count the number of times he degraded church members by saying they were "fakingly sweet," "full of themselves," "alcoholics," or his favorite "just plain ugly." If the church members knew how badly they were talked about behind closed doors, the church would have folded just a few weeks after his arrival. Both Mother and Dad were guilty of this. They dodged a huge bullet once. When my older sister was young, she had a very difficult time keeping things to herself. My mother asked her one time, "Do you ever have a thought you don't express?" She responded, "Not really." This particular Sunday after church, Mother was commenting on the service, and, in particular, the soloist. She said, "Diane sang a beautiful solo but I can't stand the way she moves her head when she sings." The next time my sister saw Diane, she inaccurately related the message, "My mother said she couldn't stand you." I am not sure how my parents recovered from that communication error, but they were much more careful about what they said in my sister's presence – except when discussing my upcoming first year at school. My sister also managed to alienate our family from our next-door neighbor who was a first-grade school teacher. Our neighbor, Ms. Crabby, as she was affectionately called, was the kind of person who would yell at little children (us) to stay out of her yard. I just don't understand why she had a problem with our picking flowers from her yard and forming a beautiful, colorful bouquet of fresh flowers to lovingly present to our mother. My parents just causally mentioned one time that they hoped I did not get Ms. Crabby for my teacher. My sister found the first opportunity to tell our neighbor just that. "Mother said she hoped Mara doesn't get you as a teacher," she said mockingly. The clever neighbor countered that she hoped the same thing.

My mother was from Alabama, and we never missed an opportunity to make fun of their accents. Of course, we hated when others made fun of ours. But, that is what our family did. We would drawl even more than usual and pronounce vowels differently to mock Mother's family. She would join in. Occasionally, we were admonished and reminded that it was not nice to make fun of people, but laughter following a particularly precise impression would be a more powerful motivator.

One particular year on the way to Alabama, our family stopped at Six Flags over Georgia, a large amusement park just outside of Atlanta. On the way back to the car, there was a deluge, and we did not have any rain protection. So, we all were completely drenched by the time we reached the car. We were also famished. My father's philosophy was that truck stops were the best bet for good food, so we stopped at the first truck stop we came across. We could tell it was a truck stop because it had a neon sign flashing "Truck Stop." My father based the quality of unknown restaurants on the number of patrons, particularly truck drivers. "Truck drivers like good food," was his rationale. This one did have a few cars and 18 wheelers in the parking lot, so we stopped. Just as we were seated, a waitress promptly approached our table with four glasses of water. When she realized there were five in our family, she said, in the most Southern drawl I have ever heard, "I didn't see but four of ya'll so I only brought four glasses of water." The wonderful day at the amusement park and the unexpected rain that had completely soaked us had left me, a very young teenager, in a particularly whimsical mood, so I snickered, knew I was going to lose it, and excused myself so I could burst out laughing without doing so right in front of the woman. It was pretty obvious that the other family members were equally amused. My father, obviously embarrassed, said, "You will have to forgive us, we have just been to Six Flags and they have the giggles." Trying to change the course of the conversation, he asked, "Have you ever been?" "Naw, and I ain't a going neither. I've seen too many people that have come from thar," was her most clever retort.

ADVANTAGES TO BEING A PREACHER'S KID

DURING MY CHILDHOOD YEARS, we lived in a parsonage that was located beside the church my father pastored. There were very distinct advantages to living beside the church. The biggest advantage was that the yard was huge. We had tons of space to play baseball, football, basketball, etc. We had about 75 yards (the length of the church) for our play space, so we had ample room to convert that space into a baseball field or football field (soccer was not yet popular), and still had room for a basketball goal. One favorite pasttime of ours was just to see how many times we could run around the church without collapsing.

Because the church was rarely locked completely, we also had access to the huge playground inside. Our church was enormous, and had many secret closets, passageways and doors ripe for exploring. My father would admonish us, "Churches are not for playing," but he didn't seem too serious about it. Hide-and seek was particularly time-consuming since there were so many potential hiding places. Sliding down the bannisters was also fun.

My older sister discovered a way to get on top of the church. If my father had caught us doing that, we would have been in deep trouble, because it truly was very dangerous. She would go up there to "lay out" in the sun. It was perfect if one wanted solitude and isolation, because she was visible only from the air. My younger sister and I ventured up there several times but realized that it was too dangerous to be climbing around on top of the church.

Another advantage of living near the church is that we no longer had to all get ready and be there at one time as we had in the previous church. But even more advantageous is that we could leave when we wanted after the services were over. That was particularly helpful since Dad had to greet all church members and would sometimes talk for hours after the service had concluded. One particular night, I remember Mother telling me to tell my older sister, who was barely a teenager at the time, that the Beatles were going to be on The Ed Sullivan Show. I had no idea what she was talking about, but relayed the message as instructed. When I told my sister, she started jumping up and down screaming, "Oh, my God!" and ran home frantic to get a first glimpse of this group. I just remember thinking how silly it seemed that the girls watching the band were screaming, crying, yelling, and some were so over-stimulated they actually fainted. I just couldn't understand how anyone could get so excited over a few boys singing.

Dad knew the church could be a frightening place, and delighted in terrifying us. One time when I thought my sister and I were the only ones in the church, I reached into another room - without looking, to turn off the lights as we were leaving, and my father brushed my arm with his hand. I yelled and told my sister to run. When we got out of the church, my father appeared, laughing hysterically.

When we were out for the evening and entered the dark house upon our return, my father also liked to tell us to, "Look under the beds to make sure nobody came in the house while we were gone." Of course, as obedient children, we would do as we were told. He would stand right behind us and yell "Boo!" very loudly as soon as we lifted the cover to peek under the bed. Thankfully, we were bright enough that he was only able to do that about 20 times before we caught on.

Sit Here!

I ADMIT, IF I allow myself, I can sometimes be an angry, white lesbian. Even though I am a small person with painfully tiny hands that I inherited from my father (I have to buy children's rings to wear on my pinky), I feel more aligned with the huge bull-dyke in spirit. And, evidently I am able to detect minute traces of discrimination and other unfair treatment to which others are completely oblivious.

When I was doing research on weddings (you'll find later in the book), I couldn't believe how many of my good, close, dyke friends had never thought about how sexist "giving the woman away" at a wedding was. I'm sure they are happier in their total lack of awareness for all things sexist. After all, ignorance really is bliss. Sometimes, I wish I could be a little (okay, a lot) more easy-going when it comes to those things. However, I also think the awareness helps me be much more sensitive to others and much less likely to treat others unfairly.

I am in a restaurant with my partner and some of her friends. There are two men and four women. I am paying the bill and I am left-handed so I always try to find a suitable seat. I sit. One of the women declared, "Ginny (who is my partner's straight friend) wants the men to sit at the head of the table." My first thought, of course, is, "I don't care what Ginny wants." I look at my partner who has these pleading eyes as if to say, "Please, don't make a big deal out of this." I decide not to, for her sake. Maybe no one else understands the symbolism. Maybe I am too obsessive about it.

As a Director of Exceptional Children, we are taught that when meeting with parents, it is important to prepare the room so everyone will be on the "same level." We are encouraged to use round tables so there is no table head, and insure that all the seats are the same height. It seems some counties would intentionally try to intimidate parents by forcing them to sit in much lower chairs, while the educators loomed large over them. So, there is no doubt that I am concerned, maybe overly so, about seating arrangements.

But, I ask you – why should men sit at the head of the table? It's a rhetorical question, naturally, since there is absolutely no logical answer. But, in case you haven't really thought about it before, the seat at the head of the table does signify the head of the household. Some may argue that men are generally bigger and, therefore, need the extra room found at the heads of the table. I could perhaps buy that point, if the larger people consistently sat at the table ends. There are certainly biblical references supporting men as the heads of the household. There are also biblical references that say it is okay to beat your slave and smash babies against rocks, but thankfully, we don't believe this in our "modern" world.

I also have a difficult time believing that some people who grew up in the 70's and 80's are still inclined towards strictly-defined roles. It just doesn't appear very imaginative to me.

I am also a little perturbed that I have not one single family member who advocates for gay rights. One of my co-worker's sisters is a lesbian, and he is vocally supportive of gay rights. I wish I had a sibling, a cousin, a parent, an aunt, uncle, nephew - **anybody** who vocally supported the gay rights movement. They are either opposed or silent on the matter, even though I attempted to solicit support from the one I thought would be the most open.

I also resent that my family didn't actively confront the sexism that was continuously encountered in my young life. I wanted to be a paper girl but girls were not allowed. I could ride a bike and throw as well as anyone. Neither could girls be crossing guards at school. I now see parents advocating so strongly for their children, and think that mine should have recognized the injustice and fought for my right to have a job. But, they didn't. I am certain that they did not want to "make waves" and jeopardize their "good standing" in the community by advocating for those "liberal" causes. Plus, as staunch Free Will Baptists, they believed in the literal interpretation of the Bible, and the Bible makes grandiose distinctions between the roles of women and men. They probably also believed that girls should not be a paper girl or a crossing guard. I am just glad there were those brave souls out there who did advocate for equal opportunities for women, and who were instrumental in societal changes for the better. I certainly don't thank God for the good old days.

WHAT DOES HE DO?

WHILE MY PARENTS WERE visiting for Christmas (and that's another whole chapter), my neighbors came over. They are a wonderful, heterosexual couple who are often described by others as the "nicest people I've ever met." I truly love them. They are liberal-minded in most things, intelligent, caring, and sensitive and, unlike my parents (particularly my father) they love animals. After they left, (during which time they received quite a few sermons from my father, who can't talk intelligently about anything except religion), my mother asked, "What does he do?"

He's a retired FBI agent," I answered. "Oh," she said, obviously impressed.

After a few seconds, I said, "You never asked what she does." She begrudgingly obliged.

I have noticed on numerous occasions that my parents notice and remember the occupations of men and seem completely disinterested in those of their spouses. And that is the way women are viewed – as the spouses of the men. One of my jobs at Thanksgiving is the get the Christmas cards ready for Mother. I lose sleep over the sexism. The labels read, "Mr. and Mrs. Walter Smith," "Mr. and Mrs. Raymond Jones," etc. I told mother the woman's name is not Walter. She doesn't get it. However, if I call her by my father's first name, Earl, she does get a little riled.

I am a school psychologist by trade who later became the Director of Exceptional Children (including gifted). My parents, who always made fun of anyone and anything who was different, didn't seem to want to acknowledge that I helped coordinate services for students with disabilities, but they were quick to tell others that I worked with gifted students. I guess they asked me about five times what I did, since they could never remember – after all, the occupations of women are not important. They, however, knew the complete history of the occupations of my brothers-in-law. They still have no idea what my partner does, but if we were married, and she were a man, they would know all the intimate details.

In all fairness to them, they did teach us to treat others fairly. We were taught the golden rule and many times were told to think about how our behaviors impacted others.

One particular Valentine's Day, when the tradition in grade school was to give Valentines to classmates, I was going to omit someone because I didn't like him. Mother said, "What if you looked around the room and saw that other people received all these valentines and you didn't get any. How would you feel?" Of course, Mother and Daddy were the most controlling people I have ever met, so feelings were negligible. So, the valuable lesson was followed by an order – "If you don't give him one, you don't give anyone one."

When integration first evolved in the South and I found that I was having one Black student in my 6th grade class, my father directed, "Now, you better be nice to her." He added, "You don't have to be best friends, just be nice." When I think about it, it is hard to believe that this is the same man who now complains incessantly that the Blacks and Mexicans are taking over the country. It is heart-warming that he was able to separate his racist opinions and far-right political leanings to have compassion for a girl who, I suppose, was faced with the daunting and perhaps terrifying challenge of being the only Black child in a classroom filled with sons and daughters of bigoted parents.

Spare the Rod

◆◆◆◆◆◆◆◆◆◆◆◆◆◆◆◆◆◆◆◆◆◆◆◆◆◆◆◆◆◆◆◆◆◆

SPEAKING OF CONTROLLING – Mother and Daddy believed in the literal application of biblical principals – the parts that made sense to them anyway. They chose to ignore the parts about eating certain things, wearing certain things, and not killing (since they believed in war and capital punishment). They really believed in spare the rod and spoil the child. Physical punishment was the order of the day. If we didn't do what was expected, we were shaken, slapped, hit, grabbed, etc. Mother would make us retrieve our own switches if she were calm enough. Otherwise she used whatever she could grab to "tear our legs up." I still despise weeping willow trees because those branches were the switches used when we visited our grandmother. I would love to have had grandparents who spoiled us – just a little – but our grandmothers were more authoritarian than our parents.

When I was about ten years old, I remember spending a Sunday afternoon with Francis, a vivacious, bubbly, petite girl who was just a little older than I was. Everyone loved her witty, charming personality. As we were playing, the subject of spanking arose. She said she had never been spanked. I was incredulous. I asked what her parents did when she did something wrong. "They talk to me," she replied. "If I do something really bad, I may be put on restriction."

She was a very well-behaved, deeply admired person by her peers. I longed for a life free from physical punishment.

If we really did something bad, Dad would make us take our pants off, lay across the bed and he would spank us with his belt. I heard my parents briefly state, almost with a disconcerting bragging tone, that in today's world, social services would have taken us. I was quite obstinate (as if you had not guessed by now), so I was hit almost every day. The trouble is, with all the good disciplinary strategies that have proven to be more effective than corporal punishment; that are more likely to produce well adjusted, responsible adults; my mother and father still believe hitting is the most effective way to discipline children. When I was much older and I was discussing child-rearing techniques with my Dad, he was, again defending the practice of corporal punishment. "Spare the rod and spoil the child," he quoted with a grin. I pointed out to him that the Bible also says, "Be not harsh with your children, lest they rebel." That just made him angry.

My parents also wanted to control who I dated. A guy from our church was interested in me and asked me out. My parents told me his parents would get the impression that I thought I was better than he was if I didn't date him. So, I did. It actually turned out to be a lot of fun. I had never had any alcohol or smoked pot until that date. Maybe Mama does know best.

With their strict, rigid rules and controlling personalities, they won the battle, but lost the war. I'll never be emotionally close to my parents. I see in them controlling people who firmly believe I'm going to hell because I'm gay. Every time Dad speaks about the doctrine he believes in, I'm reminded that he thinks I am going to hell.

My sister, who is almost as evangelical as my parents (but fails to realize it), told me one time my homosexuality must be a form of rebellion. Yes, I have this undeniable attraction to women because my parents were too strict. That's as ridiculous as the antiquated and ridiculous theory that autism is caused by emotionally frigid mothers. This same sister refused to participate in yoga because she thought it was associated with Buddhism, and would ultimately lead to a conversion to Buddhism. Both my sisters, however, have come around, as have other people, to realize that homosexuality is truly beyond our control, and we should be accepted and valued. I have no idea how they feel now about gay marriage. No one in my family has been outspoken in support of it, or, in my presence at least, been vocally opposed.

But, with all that said, I have to give my Mother credit for the book incident. At least, she was reading a book that helped her understand. At least, she was trying to get information – unlike my father. My father believed that everything he needed to learn, he learned at Duke in the 1940s. We tried to get him to learn to use the computer. He was not interested. We tried to get him to take a Spanish class. "English is all I need to know. If people can't speak English, they do not need to come into this country," he complained. He will not try ethnic restaurants because he doesn't like "that foreign mess."

I have to say, however, for an evangelical family – they've done better than expected about accepting – maybe tolerating is the better word – my lesbianism. After I told my sister that Ramona was my family, and I would appreciate if her Christmas presents were a little better – and after I told my parents that we were sleeping in the same bed in their house, or we would go to a motel – they did better.

Naturally, I could have never come out to them (even if I had come out to myself) before adulthood. I wasn't sure of the reaction and thought that my plight may become as I had seen others – being thrown out of their house. I didn't relish being homeless and uneducated, so I had to make sure I was able to live independently before I was comfortable with too much sharing. That way, I couldn't be thrown out of the house.

My move was to just avoid them as much as possible. I only went "home" when I was in college when the dorms closed and I had no other place to go. Being in their house, under their strict rule was like being in jail. My younger friends had much less strict curfews and rules.

As an example of their strictness, we were not allowed to go to the movies until I was in 6th grade and only Disney movies were allowed at that time. When my other friends talked about good movies they had seen, I could not relate. I had to pretend I was sick one Sunday night when I was 13 to watch the Wizard of Oz on television. It always came on Sunday nights, and since we had church, we always missed it. I think Mother was glad I was "sick" because she seemed to enjoy watching it, too.

Since my parents were so strict when I was in high school, I had little knowledge of the "ways of the world." So my college experience was challenging and unique. When my parents were first moving me into the dorms, they noticed that the girls beside me had beer they were stocking in their room. They said, "Oh my, there are alcoholics living beside you."

They also heard, mistakenly, that I had started drinking beer. This was not true, only because I did not like beer. I did try it, but never liked the taste. I preferred liquor and wine. When they told me someone had reported that I was drinking beer, I honestly told them that I did not drink beer. I admitted, as was true, that I had tasted it and could not stand the taste. They seemed satisfied. I realized that was "splitting hairs" with the truth, but the alternative – I could not even imagine the alternative.

My first experience with wine was remarkable. I drank about one fourth of a glass and got a nice buzz. "Wow, I bet if I drank the whole bottle, I would really feel good," I thought. It doesn't take a genius to figure out, very quickly, that it doesn't work that way. Mark it up to my naivety.

Gambling

OUR FAMILY MOVED FROM Wilson to New Bern, North Carolina while I was in the second grade. I realized quickly that the school curricula were different. I had no knowledge of cursive writing. My previous school did not teach that until third grade. My first memorable experience in my new school was a classmate "telling" the teacher that I was printing instead of "writing." I was always one of the top students in the class, so that was the first time I felt academically inadequate.

I made up for my inadequacies, however, when introduced to a new game, Marbles. I was taught to play and, because of my prowess, was instantly the envy and bane of other players. I was excited that I had won so many of the other students' marbles. I could not wait to get home and tell my parents how skilled I was and to show them the result of my superiority in this new game – the marbles I had won from all the other students. The paper bag in which I had lovingly stored these precious gems was exploding with the weight. I proudly displayed my wares only to hear my father, with the typical scowl on his face bark emphatically, "That is gambling and that is a sin. You take those marbles and give every one of them back." I was devastated. I would have to part with my precious winnings. More importantly, I had really expected that my father would be proud that

I was good at something I had just learned. Instead, I was treated with contempt and criticism.

Years later, I was very surprised when my parents announced they were going to Las Vegas. Their attitude towards gambling had not changed, but they heard the food was good and the shows were fabulous. They loved to eat and be entertained. This same man who refused to darken the doors of any place that sold alcohol a few years earlier was going to Las Vegas? Actually, they loved it.

Their least favorite vacation was their cruise to the Bahamas. When they complained about that vacation, I questioned, "You don't like the beach, you don't like to drink, you don't like to dance, you don't like to swim, you don't like to fish. What made you think you would like the Bahamas?" They argued that almost everyone they have talked to said they like the Bahamas. I countered, "Those people like the beach, and they like to drink, dance, swim and fish."

FAMILY AND MARRIAGE

◆◇◆◇◆◇◆◇◆◇◆◇◆◇◆◇◆◇◆◇◆◇◆◇◆◇◆◇◆◇◆◇◆◇◆◇

SPEND ONLY A COUPLE of minutes with a heterosexual couple and you are sure to hear the words "family" and "marriage." My partner and I decided a long time ago that we would encourage others to acknowledge us as "family." When my 7 year old nephew, speaking about my partner, announced, "She's not family," I declared emphatically, "She is, too." (That was such a sophisticated, compelling argument).

Holidays and funerals, however, seem to drive us relentlessly into reality. Even though we successfully stayed together during Christmas for the first 24 years of our relationship, stubbornly refusing to separate because nobody else would expect their husband and wife to separate during Christmas, reality hit hard when my partner's mother lost her spouse very close to Christmas. No one wanted her to stay by herself on Christmas Eve and Christmas Day so, of course, since she wasn't "married," my partner was elected unanimously, to spend the time with her. My parents had already planned to spend Christmas with us. This was a dilemma with no acceptable solution and, certainly, no winners. I felt for my partner's mother, and naturally, I didn't want her to spend Christmas by herself, either. The only solution was for us to part. The reality that we truly are not family by anyone's standards hit hard and furiously. It was, quite frankly, the worst Christmas I ever had. I couldn't shake the depressing, very sinking feeling that, no matter how hard we try, we are just fooling ourselves by thinking we are family. I wasn't listed in my partner's mother's husband's obituary, and I'm sure she won't be listed on anything my family has to offer. That is one of the reasons, I firmly believe, that people oppose gay marriage. If we were married, we would be family – legally and without a doubt in anyone's minds. But without that piece of paper, no matter how we act, no matter how much we protest, no matter how much we try to help people understand, we are not each other's family.

We have minimal protections in some states if we make the effort to ensure that all legal documents are in place. But death and money drive some people beyond the brink of what we think they are capable, so we did not hesitate to make sure we were legally protected.

Marriage is such an important rite of passage into adulthood, the same nephew mentioned above asked me when I was going to grow up. I was about 40 at the time. I answered, "I am grown." "But, you are not married," he protested. When adults talk about their children, their marital status is almost one of the first things mentioned. Some parents spend more money on their children's weddings than they do their educations.

Speaking of money on weddings – one thing that definitely worked to my advantage was that my refusal to marry saved my parents so much money they offered to pay my graduate school tuition. Actually, the statement was, "Either we will pay for your graduate school or your marriage, but we can't afford both." That was the easiest decision I've ever had to make in my life. I hope I have been generous enough with gifts I have bought for them that they feel the money spent on my graduate school tuition was a good investment for them. I also know that graduate school assured me a good career and allowed financial independence. I was very grateful for their financial assistance and support, but I would have starved before I would have asked them for additional assistance, or moved back in with them.

One last thought on families – I tense when I hear people say, "We are trying to start a family." Translated, that means, "We are trying to have a child." So, when did children become the sole ingredient for the definition of family? My partner and I are family, even without children. Heterosexual couples are family once they declare themselves as such – with or without children. The traditional definition of family has, thankfully, changed for the better.

PAYBACK IS HEAVEN

◇◇◇◇◇◇◇◇◇◇◇◇◇◇◇◇◇◇◇◇◇◇◇◇◇◇◇◇◇◇◇◇◇◇◇◇◇◇

DESPITE THE FACT THAT we were physically beaten and over-controlled, there were some great things about my parents. One of my fondest memories was that they would often let us drive the car on dirt roads on Sunday afternoons so we would be good drivers when we did get our licenses. Of course, after the first time we were allowed to do that, we begged and pleaded every Sunday for them to let us drive.

When he was in his 70's, my father had a horrible battle with cancer and lost his driver's license because the medication he was taking made him very groggy. Naturally, that was very difficult for him. When he came to my house for Christmas, I took him on a back road and let him drive. He said it felt great to be behind the wheel again. Payback really can be heaven!

Of course, my father was never the best driver in the world. His philosophy was, "The other guy better watch out for me. Bicyclists and pedestrians should stay off the road, because the road was made for cars." One day in particular, he was driving even more aggressively and recklessly than usual, since we were late to school. He was tailgating a car that stopped to turn, and he plowed into the back of the other car. Although my sister and I were told to stay in the car so we could not hear what was said, the other woman must have been fussing about how closely he was following. He claimed she was a witch (not to her face, of course). He, the infallible Reverend, ended up with the citation, and I ended up later being very good friends with the woman's daughter. Dad always referred to the woman he had hit as a busybody and a witch. I think he had probably never encountered a woman who was not afraid to stand up to him before. I am certain he felt vindicated in his own mind that the wreck indeed was her fault after all; for why should she have slowed down when it was obvious that he was in such a hurry?

My father loved to laugh and tell, what we usually considered to be, corny jokes. He often told jokes that were offensive and racist, although I never heard him use profanity. Profanity, it seems, was forbidden, even sinful, although it seemed perfectly acceptable to call someone the "N" word. I was so tired of hearing the 'N" word and kept trying to explain to him that it was very offensive, rude and ignorant. Nothing I said made a difference, so I tried a new approach. One day, he let the "N" word fly and I responded, "I hate that damn word." He gasped and said, "Mara, you watch your mouth." I told him that most people think the "N" word is much worse than "damn" so every time he used the "N" word, I was going to say "damn." I never heard him use it again.

Of course, I was an adult at the time. Had I tried this when I was a child, I would probably still be peeling my face off the wall.

QUALITATIVE STUDY OF DYKE'S PERCEPTIONS OF WEDDINGS

THERE IS NO DOUBT that my family thinks I am strange. Sometimes I wonder how I was born into such a family in the first place. My parents are Baptist fundamentalists and my sisters have followed suit. They all seem to love dressing up and going to church. I remember my sisters, when they were pre-teens talking about getting married and having babies. "I'm never getting married," I declared, emphatically.

"You'll change your mind," most people advised. Frankly, part of it was that I was too scared my Mother's wish would come true. "I hope you have a daughter just like you so you'll know how I feel," she would say when she was exasperated with me. So, I decided a long time ago – I was not getting married and I was certainly having no babies.

I wondered why I was felt so different and didn't realize why until I was well into college. Then the realization hit me like a ton of bricks. Let me digress.

I was always a little masculine. I preferred guns to dolls and liked playing baseball instead of playing "house." I loved my baseball cap but would go "ballistic" when Easter came around and I had to wear a more feminine hat. I hated wearing dresses and hose, and hated carrying purses around – although they did tend to come in handy if you felt compelled to hit someone. I found if you put a brick in it, it made a very nice weapon.

I remember seeing an acquaintance of mine – a fellow basketball player and one who was more masculine than I – with her mother shopping. She looked as happy as I felt. Her mother was trying to get her to try on hats and she was arguing and yelling and crying. I certainly was empathetic. If only someone would understand how we felt and not try to mold us into what everyone else thinks we need to be.

But, that never happened. I had to play the game – grin and bear it. While my family thought I was ridiculous and selfish, I thought I was very giving and accommodating by not yelling and screaming every time I felt like it – every Sunday to be exact. Then when my sisters actually did get married and I was "supposed" to be in the weddings, I thought I would never live through it. I did not tell them since I didn't want to spoil the wedding for them – but I would have rather done just about anything than be in a wedding party. I think all my family thought it was very funny watching me – feeling like a true drag queen – trying to impersonate a feminine person who actually enjoyed being in the wedding party. I only made it through each one by pretending to be an actor in a movie about a wedding.

Numerous heterosexual people, including my family, have looked at me like I was a freak when I talked about my dislike for weddings. Since most women enjoy weddings immensely, they can't imagine somebody not liking them. I started wondering myself – is it just me, or are there other people who despise these formal, church weddings as much as I do?

The invitation that lay on the counter created excessive anxiety before it was opened. I knew the content – an invitation to a church wedding. Maybe I'll get in some accident and not be able to go. Maybe some tragedy will resolve me of my obligation to attend my nephew's wedding.

I had rather have some tragedy than go to a wedding? Was there something wrong with me? Most people seemed to enjoy weddings. Maybe it was a dyke thing. I decided to find out.

During the time I started to research this, I was in a doctoral program and wondering what I was going to do for my dissertation. Funny, when you are in a doctoral program, everyone always asks, "What are you going to do your dissertation on?" (I resist the temptation to correct the grammar.) I guess doing a study of dyke's perceptions of weddings wouldn't exactly contribute to the body of knowledge on educational leadership. However, I was so interested in why I was so averse to weddings, and wondered if it truly is a "dyke thing." I figured I needed a diversion from the grueling work required of a dissertation, so I persisted.

In my first recollection of a wedding – I was a flower girl. Maybe it was the fact that I threw flower petals overhand – hard - at the wedding guests that resulted in this being my only engagement. Let's face it, dainty, I wasn't (and am not).

Later, when I was old enough to know better, I tried to avoid weddings because I hated dressing up, as many dykes do. Our mothers just never understood that dressing up was (and is) torture. Wearing feminine clothes makes me feel like a drag queen. (Of course, I can only guess how drag queens must feel.)

One would have to be blind and deaf to miss the obvious attraction heterosexual women have to formal weddings. Every heterosexual woman I interviewed said they loved weddings, loved to dress up, and loved to see the young people who were obviously so in love in weddings. These people had an expression of absolute ecstasy when talking about weddings. I just cannot relate to these women who said they loved socializing with other people and even enjoyed watching weddings on television.

On a scale of 1 to 5 with 1 being torture and 5 being the best thing every - the heterosexual women unanimously rated weddings as a 5. The highest score received from a gay woman was a 2. One liked the reception okay but hated the church part, and, naturally, hated dressing up.

One, who talked about weddings as if I were self-recording my disdain for these ceremonies, rated it a .5. She said she feels out of place and has nothing in common with the people who attend weddings. To her, weddings are a big show, everyone is partnered, and she feels out of place, particularly at the reception. Someone once said that some heterosexual had complained that gays shouldn't be allowed to have gay pride parades since heterosexuals don't have anything comparable. "Of course they do," he argued, "weddings." I agree – formal church weddings seem to epitomize what one would expect at a heterosexual parade.

Another respondent argued that the money spent on weddings is outrageous. "Spending $25,000 on a wedding instead of a down payment on a house is ridiculous," she insisted. She added, "I like receptions as long as it is not in a church." Her partner stated that she would rather go to a funeral than attend a wedding. So, I'm not alone in my thinking.

It was funny that many people, including dykes, had not thought that the tradition of women being escorted down the aisle and "given away" was very old-fashioned and symbolized possession. Once they realized that brides were traditionally given by their families to their new husbands, they were upset about it, too.

Most dykes indicated that they never dreamed of weddings when they were little girls, unlike the heterosexual women, and they didn't enjoy watching weddings on TV. One heterosexual woman admitted that love of weddings is a "girly" thing.

In her book, *Sex, Lies and Stereotypes*, Kim Ficera describes my attitude towards weddings most eloquently when she states, "I'd rather be a silent mourner at an Italian wake, when the widow wails for three solid days while clutching what's left of the salami her husband choked to death on, than suffer through a traditional wedding." (p. 130).

Yep, that just about wraps it up!

WHY DYKES DON'T CARRY PURSES

DYKES HAVE NEVER RELISHED typical feminine things. Some wear make-up, others don't, some carry purses, others don't. Dykes like pants with pockets, so they are able to carry any necessities in their pockets or in their socks, whichever fits better. Many dykes carry purses only when absolutely necessary – when they have too much stuff to cram in pockets and socks. Others never carry purses, but substitute things like backpacks if absolutely necessary. But why don't dykes carry purses, and why don't I carry a purse? I'm not really sure. Maybe it's a statement akin to a secret handshake. "Look at that woman; she's kind of dyky-looking. Oh, but she has a purse – must not be a dyke."

I think dykes view purses as people with bodily identity integrity disorder view their limbs. Most people, in their wildest dreams, could not understand "amputee wannabees" - those people who feel they cannot be "whole" unless one of their appendages is surgically removed. I think dykes are probably the only cluster of people who may have a deep appreciation and understanding of that disorder. Purses just feel like an appendage that needs to be surgically removed.

Why Dykes Don't Have Babies

SOME LESBIANS WANT CHILDREN. Many of us, however, truthfully assert that we have never, ever had a maternal instinct in our lives. When I was five, as a last-ditch effort to persuade me toward the more feminine things, my parents bought me a doll for Christmas. I, of course, had not asked for a doll. I had, however, asked for guns and a cowboy hat. I expressed excitement over the guns I had wanted, but never touched the doll. I never had a thing to do with it. When my parents asked if I liked the doll, I exclaimed emphatically, "No, I didn't want a doll." At no time in my life did I ever express a wish for a doll or a human baby. Many dykes have pets, and that seems to fulfill most of our parental desires.

WHY DYKES MAKE SUCH
GREAT EMPLOYEES

◇◇◇◇◇◇◇◇◇◇◇◇◇◇◇◇◇◇◇◇◇◇◇◇◇◇◇◇◇◇◇◇◇◇◇◇

IF YOU WANT A good worker, hire a dyke. Naturally, that is not
100% accurate, for we are just as diverse as heterosexuals and gay
men. However, all my friends are very intelligent, dedicated, well-
respected, and extremely hard-working employees.

One thing that sets us apart is that we don't have husbands and
most of don't have children, so our responsibilities at home may not
be as demanding. Therefore, we have more time to devote to our
jobs. Another thing is that the employer doesn't have to worry about
sexual harassment charges with lesbians. Lesbians, with their body
language, (okay maybe the masculine appearance has something to
do with it, too) typically don't invite sexual overtures. If a man is
too dense and continues his pursuit, lesbians usually don't have any
problem telling him to "back off." A heterosexual woman may not
be as assertive.

WHY DYKES WEAR MEN'S CLOTHES

I KNOW THERE ARE some dykes who are criticized openly or privately (or behind the back) for preferring men's clothes. For one thing, since women don't carry purses, we need good pockets. Men's pants have much better (deeper and bigger) pockets than women's clothes. Men's clothes are typically cheaper than women's clothes as well.

Many dykes just don't like frilly clothes with lace and low necklines. Men's clothes don't typically have those features. And, let's face it; some dykes are built more like men than women anyway, so the clothes just fit better.

Disclaimer – Some people do not like the term "dyke" at all. My apologies to anyone who may be offended. I use this term only in the most endearing way.

Life Goals – Doctorate, Black Belt, and Book Writing

◇◇◇◇◇◇◇◇◇◇◇◇◇◇◇◇◇◇◇◇◇◇◇◇◇◇

MY THREE AMBITIOUS LIFE goals were to get a doctorate, a black belt in karate, and to have a book published. I have the doctorate and hope this book thing works out. However, karate is a different story.

I had wanted to take karate since I was a child, and I developed a serious crush on Honey West. *Honey West* was a TV show starring two detectives who were married (I think), and were karate experts. They both could put someone to sleep with a quick jab to the neck. I really wanted to be able to do that. (Okay, so I have power and control issues.) I begged Dad to let me take karate lessons. He finally took me to a martial arts school and discussed it. The instructor told us the classes were on Monday and Wednesday nights. Unfortunately, since we were Baptists, Wednesday night was designated for "Prayer Meeting" and since I was the minister's daughter, there was no way I could take karate on a Wednesday night. The instructor didn't seem to think paying the monthly fee (that evidently wasn't negotiable) and attending classes only one day a week would provide the proper training for me. Therefore, my dreams of being a martial arts expert were resentfully dashed.

One of the first things I did when I was released from my parents' rules, and had the money to afford to make my own decisions was to enroll in a karate school. I took for many years. My sensei, Tola Lewis, who was the fiercest fighter one hoped never to face, was a wonderful, supportive, encouraging man. I took lessons from him when I was in my late 30's. An adolescent, who was also taking it with me, had just completed a kata demonstration in front of the entire class. "You're entering that gangly stage," Sensei told him. I was next. I was in my 30's at the time. After I finished, Sensei laughed as he told me, "You're entering that gangly stage." I never bragged about my sense of balance and coordination. My mother said when I was young, I would walk right off the porch into the bushes. After I related that story to one of my childhood friends who loved to give people nicknames, I became thereafter known as "Bushy."

After years of hard work and practicing, I did obtain brown belt status, and was very proud of that accomplishment. My venture into karate helped me better understand people who had learning differences, for I was far from a natural. I knew what I wanted to do, but my stiff, uncoordinated joints just wouldn't cooperate. I did love the katas and the physical workouts, but eventually, my instructor started focusing on a form of judo, and I decided I was too old to be thrown to the floor 20 times in one night. But, I will always have a very deep appreciation for the skills and discipline I learned under this great Sensei's tutelage.

I am not sure where my deep desire to earn a doctorate arose – most likely – my mother. She did try to push us all, and would make comments about having a doctor in the family. Sometimes I think if I had not been shaken so much in my mother's fits of anger and frustration, I may have had the brains to be a medical doctor. My only chance of getting into medical school now is as a cadaver. I often dreamed of being super intelligent – you know – Rachel

Maddow smart. Deprived of super-intelligence by both nature and nurture, however, I at least did have the motivation to achieve to my maximum potential. In psychological terms, I had a deep drive towards self-actualization.

When I was in middle school, I said I wanted to be an optometrist. That is because I loved my optometrist, Dr. Chitty, who was very friendly, and thanks to his interventions, helped me see better. He was very well-respected in the community, and I thought he performed a great service to people. I was fascinated with the machines in his office, and thought it would be great to help other people see better. Then, I met my 9th grade biology teacher, who really turned me off to science. She droned on in a monotonous voice that would have lulled a person high on crystal meth right to sleep. I decided I hated science and everything connected to it (which is such a shame because I am now fascinated with all aspects of science), so my dreams of a career in optometry were laid to rest.

I had no targeted career path after that. I was fascinated with foreign language, and loved French, but realized that teaching was probably the only career a major in that would allow, and I did not want to teach. So, I was stressed about not knowing what I was going to do when I grew up. This consternation was quite concerning to me because for years, I had a plan and felt comfort in knowing what my life's work was going to be. It was all laid out and ultimately destroyed. So, I needed to develop a new plan. I knew I didn't want to teach, or be a nurse – I did not have the compassion for sick people, and really didn't want to deal with all those bodily fluids. I felt confident that I would find something and be successful. But I couldn't help but worry that I may end up homeless, on the streets of New York City with all the other failures - or, even worse, in my parents' house. So, I did some very hard thinking, knowing that if I thought hard and long enough, I could solve this problem, and discover my new life's plan.

When I finally got to college, I fell in love with psychology. This, I thought, was the key to helping people. This would enable me to uncover deep, dark secrets lurking inside peoples' minds that would, with my expert assistance, unravel to allow them to lead successful, problem-free lives for eternity. I thought I was going to be the best thing since Freud himself, and discover some unbelievably significant breakthrough that would contribute enormously to the field – and help numerous people become more emotionally stable.

So, I majored in psychology and we all know where a Bachelor's degree in psychology gets us. Yes, I worked at a restaurant waiting tables. My other choice was a psych ward making minimum wage. I decided very quickly I needed a different career path, although I really appreciated the restaurant owner for making this work available to me. I am, without doubt, not a great waitress. Good, perhaps, but not great. I was efficient and fast, but I have a more professional than a friendly, flirty approach that is valued in fast-food restaurants. When men would flirt with me, it was usually quite nauseating – not flattering at all. Meanwhile, the waitresses who were natural flirters would make sufficiently more tips, but I could not bring myself to change my basic personality for a few extra dollars. My lack of coordination also did not bode well with a waitressing career. One time I spilled Brunswick stew on a little boy's head. That really wasn't my fault – my arm was bumped. Another time, I spilled hot coffee on an old man's crotch. Okay, that one was my fault, but it was not intentional.

I jumped at the chance to get my Master's and the day I received the acceptance letter into the program was, perhaps, the most exciting day of my life. I had decided that I would be a school psychologist. I loved children and knew I would never have any of my own, but wanted to be around them. I loved the funny things they said, and admired their honesty. I also thought since they were so young, they would be more amenable to the expert interventions I was going to learn and use with them.

My experience waiting tables came in handy. Although my parents, God bless them, paid for my tuition, I was responsible for everything else – room, board, books, entertainment, cigarettes, marijuana. I received a small scholarship, but mostly had to work my way through my graduate school years. I waited tables, taught undergraduate classes, and accepted as many meagerly paying internship positions as possible to survive. I even worked in tobacco one summer to avoid having to move back in with my parents for the summer. I couldn't afford anything but the most basic things, but those days taught me to appreciate the things I have now much more.

After I landed my first professional job as a psychologist, I remember riding through the county of employment and being overcome by an enormous sense of responsibility. I thought, "I am now responsible for the mental health of all the children in this county." I realize now that was far from realistic, but the anxious mind took over. I enjoyed my experiences tremendously, but soon realized that I wanted something more. Changes could really occur if I had more responsibilities, more power, more control! So, I worked my way into administration, increased my responsibilities and stress level (to an unbelievable dimension). Yet, I wanted more! I had not yet achieved the self-actualized status! I had yet to obtain a terminal degree. I hated to be introduced as Ms. Hollis when others around me were introduced as Dr. Brown or Dr. Smith. Not that there were so many of them, but I wanted to be one of those. I admired and respected those who had achieved that level. My mother's siblings had received doctorates, so I figured, if genes were any contributing factors, I could, too. That was one of those things that I thought I would regret on my death bed if I did not pursue, so I did.

The course work was interesting. It was not that cognitively challenging, just extremely time-consuming, but I enjoyed it. I liked my journey back into the world of academia, and was adequately motivated. I easily maneuvered and completed the coursework required. Even the comprehensive examinations (comps) were not that bad. The dissertation process, however, is another thing. It truly separates the women from the girls. That was the most grueling thing I had ever encountered, and it is not surprising to learn how many ABDs (All But Dissertation) are lurking in the shadows. I can't count the times I wanted to shove the volumes of research material and countless drafts through the windows and give up. I decided it would not only take persistence, but downright stubbornness to continue. I was definitely stubborn. I cannot emphasize that enough. I could not believe that my proclivity for stubbornness was the "salvation" that gave me what it takes to finish the dissertation process, but that is what it took. So, on April 26, 2010, less than three months after my mother died, I was awarded the doctorate. Since she was the only one in the immediate family who seemed so pleased that I was getting a doctorate, I was so sorry she did not live long enough to make that dream come true for her, and me. I know if she were alive, she would greet me each time I visited with, "There is Dr. Hollis." My father just laughs when he makes references to my doctorate – very typical of him. He also still addresses any letters or cards he sends to me as "Miss."

LEARNING HOW TO RIDE
A BIKE AND SWIM

◇◇◇◇◇◇◇◇◇◇◇◇◇◇◇◇◇◇◇◇◇◇◇◇◇◇◇◇◇◇◇◇

AS I HAVE ADMITTED, my sense of coordination and grace is definitely lacking. When I was five or six, my parents reluctantly removed the training wheels from my first bicycle after I begged them sufficiently. Nobody else my age still had training wheels. "She's going to kill herself," Mother warned. Mother tried to teach me, but as soon as she let go, over into the dirt I went. I heard Mother and Daddy talking one night about it. "I'm going to have to put the training wheels back on," Daddy said. "She is really going to get hurt."

I had to develop a fool-proof plan. "I'll have to show them I know how to ride. If I do that, they won't put the training wheels back on," I plotted. So, I arose early the next morning, and enlisted the assistance of my 68 year old next door neighbor, Ms. Morris. I knocked on her door, and she answered. I explained my situation, and she said she would help me. Later that morning, after 45 minutes of determined practice with the exhausted neighbor, I showed them first-hand that I could ride the bike without training wheels. Sweet SUCCESS!!!!

My mother could not swim, so she was terrified of bodies of water – pools, oceans, rivers, etc. Dad knew how to swim, but never played with us or taught us how to play any sports. Luckily, Mr. Morris (no relation to our neighbor who taught me how to ride a bike), who was one of our church members, taught me how to swim and how to ride a pony. He was a wonderfully warm, handsome man (my grandmother called him "pretty") and seemed to have the patience of Job with my klutziness. I learned how to swim and water ski under his tutelage.

My parents, of course, had all kinds of negative things to say about the Morris family. They were wealthy by other church member standards, since they had a beautiful house on the river, ponies, boats, etc. Ms. Morris wore fur coats, and dressed nicely. Their grandchild was called "the infant" and Dad would say in a mocking voice, "They call him the infant." He criticized that they were being presumptuous. I found them, however, to be very nice, friendly, helpful, and warm. And there was nothing I appreciated more than their willingness to teach me such important skills as swimming and pony riding.

Can't See the Forest

"LOOK AT ALL THOSE aggravating dandelions," my mother said with disgust and slight irritability. She had disrupted my thoughts of the beautiful surroundings. I had just moved into a beautiful, quiet neighborhood. We were taking what I thought was a wonderfully peaceful walk through the rural, wooded setting.

"I can't believe it," I confided. "I was just thinking how beautiful everything is and you are upset about the dandelions." I thought how happy I was that I had not inherited her negative and anxiety-provoking attitudes of things, not to such an extreme extent, anyway. This exchange was but one example of how our thought processes differed, and was but one more piece of evidence I possessed that made me constantly question, "How in the world could I ever have been born into this family? Me - a lesbian, born into a family of - well – evangelicals."

My parents' heaven and hell mentality had, I think, a lot to do with their bipolar view of the world. In their world, there were few uncertainties - things were clearly outlined. Either one was going to heaven, or to hell. If you were a Christian, you were going to heaven, preferably White heaven, because they weren't too fond of non-whites. If you were Jewish, Muslim or Buddhist, you didn't have a chance. I think when people with such strong beliefs think they are dying, they are bound to have at least one "what-if" thought. What if "they" are right and I am wrong? That means "they" are going to heaven and I'm going to hell. They have got to realize that not everyone can be right. So, panic sets in.

My mother actually told me the worst nightmare she ever had was that Jesus came to gather his flock in the "Rapture." She saw all her friends and family ascending into the heavens, but she stayed put. She tried jumping up and down vigorously several times, but to no avail, and realized that she had been left behind. She must have had a guilty conscious over something to have that dream. You certainly do not have to have studied Freud to analyze that dream correctly.

Dogs

PAUL MCCARTNEY SAID, "YOU can judge a man's true character by the way he treats his fellow animals." My father never met a dog he wanted to take home. He was much too obsessive about his clothes to allow a dog in his presence. When he comes to our house, he continuously tells the dogs "No" when they signal their desire to jump in his lap.

I always loved dogs and have always wanted one or two. One particular breed I wanted was a Chihuahua. When I was young, we had church members who had a Chihuahua, and she would always jump in my lap. The owners were shocked because the dog would never do that with anyone else, but would sit with me for hours and let me pet her. So, I wanted a Chihuahua when I grew up. My begging endlessly for a dog when we were young fell on deaf ears.

When I established my own household, I got a Chihuahua. One of my friends who knew I wanted a Chihuahua had an aunt who wanted to get rid of hers because she kept attacking her granddaughter. "Excellent," I thought. I love spunky animals. So, I met this animal and since she didn't immediately attack me, I felt sure we would bond. She was re-named Sombra, and was the greatest little dog. She did decide to "go there" about two weeks after I got her. She was in bed, and growled at me. I pointed my finger in her face, told her in a very stern voice she better not ever do that again, and that was all that was needed.

It seemed there was always a contest when our friends came over to see which one of them Sombra would tolerate. Two of our friends seem compelled to try to touch her at some point during their visit without Sombra's snapping at them. Sombra actually seemed to love my mother and never snapped at her. (She has never actually bitten anyone since she has been with us.) Dad, however, is another story. One time, he did allow Sombra in his lap. He was petting her repeatedly. My father is very heavy-handed and has no idea what a gentle touch is. I remember when we were younger, I hated when he tied our shoes because he always tied them much too tight. Anyway, he was petting Sombra roughly, and she snapped. That was a good excuse for him not to ever have anything to do with her again.

My father doesn't understand why anyone loves animals so much. To him, they are a nuisance, a trip hazard, and a hairy, slobbering mess. I have a hard time understanding why anyone doesn't love animals. They are loyal, loving, comforting, energetic, and so happy to see you when you return – even if you have only been gone for a few hours. To me, there is nothing like a dog. To my father, the world would be a better place without them.

Nature Lover - Right!

AFTER MY MOTHER DIED, my father chose to live by himself. There were other options but he insisted on staying home and keeping the house exactly as Mother had kept it. He would get very angry if the housekeeper or caregiver moved any objects or changed anything in the house. When asked about alternative housing options, he would emphatically declare, "The only place I'm ever moving to again is a funeral home, then a graveyard."

He was naturally lonely, although he did have someone coming to the house every day except Saturday to visit with him for at least 4 hours. During one visit, when he was feeling sorry for himself (and rightfully so), I suggested that he get outside in the sunshine more often to brighten his spirits and reap the Vitamin D benefits the sun provides. He didn't seem interested. I tried to encourage him, "You could go outside and feel the warm sun on your face, listen to the birds sing (he contorted his face in a disapproving expression), and look up into the beautiful sky." He responded, "So, you look up at the sky, and that's it. It doesn't change, so you look up and there it is. What is so nice about that?"

I had wondered why we had very rarely gone to the beach as children, and why we had never visited state parks. I sadly and painfully realized that he did not have a nature-loving bone in his body. Mother was just as bad. She never met a critter she didn't find aggravating or want to kill. My love for nature must have come through another genetic pool. Maybe my older sister was right all these years. Maybe I was adopted after all. Maybe my father was the milkman. No, that couldn't be. I have my father's scrawny arms and big ears, and my mother's penchant for industry. Thank goodness I avoided my father's loquacity. Maybe my love for nature was just a form of rebellion. After all, according to my older sister, my preference for women is.

I did manage to take Dad to a state park, Cliffs of the Neuse in Wayne County, North Carolina one time. We were reading an informational board that described how the cliffs were formed. According to the information, it took millions of years for that to happen. Being the good Christian he is, he just didn't believe that the cliffs were formed at any other time during the six days of creation, and that definitely was not millions of years ago. He harrumphed, "They can't tell how old things are."

I really pondered the reason I love nature so much and neither of my parents seem to have an appreciation for it. I have always been a pensive person. Not that my thoughts were that profound, but I do tend to think a lot. Perhaps that is why I am more reserved and quiet than many of my family members. I have thought about different religions, the reasons for our existences, what happens when we die, why we are here, what might have happened if we had taken a different route, what my life would be like if I had gone to another college – those kinds of things. Not too much different than the thoughts of an obsessive-compulsive disorder, but that is in the genes as well. My father would spend 10 minutes (no exaggeration) combing his few strands of hair, and then spray a whole bottle of hair spray (okay, slight exaggeration). My mother thoroughly cleaned her house, not only in the spring, but in the fall, winter, and summer.

Actually, we all thoroughly cleaned the house during those times. She hated when I called her "Mommie Dearest."

One thing I am happy that my mother obsessed about was table manners. I still haven't figured out how she could have put up with my father's sloppy table manners. She taught us to keep our hands in our laps. Dad spreads his long, hairy arms all over the table, and seems to like to grab our things. Mother taught us to keep our hands to ourselves. Mother also taught us to chew our food thoroughly and not talk when we had food in our mouths. Dad never got that memo. When he thinks of something to say, he is going to say it whether he has just crammed his mouth full or not. It is really gross to sit across from him during a meal. He invades your space with his arms and with his half-chewed food flying from his mouth. He doesn't seem to understand hints (modeling by not talking until I have swallowed, or my references to the bad manners others have because they don't keep their hands in their laps). All those attempts just fly right over his head. He does seem to try, however, if we go to nicer places and I remind us all ahead of time that we all need to use our best manners. I have to make specific recommendations like, "We all have to remember to keep our hands in our laps and not chew with our mouths open or talk with food in our mouths." Dad seems to be able to comply for that one night, but he apparently has no generalization skills.

As a result of my profound thoughts, I have successfully solved most of the secrets of the universe. Therefore, I have no patience for people who continue to cling to outdated ideas that "God" has a hand in everything. What kind of a God would "create" this helpless child who can't move anything on his body but his eyeballs? What kind of God would thrust a brain cancer on a 2-year old while their horrified parents watched her writhing in pain? What kind of God would force a child to become severely autistic to the point that he banged himself in the head until he bled; or kicked, scratched and bit anyone, including his mother, who attempted to help or comfort him? What kind of God would allow a little child to be horribly sexually abused? I have no patience for people like my father who told Mother he prayed that she would get a good report from the doctor – therefore taking responsibility for the good report she received – only two weeks prior to the cancer diagnosis. I never heard him taking blame for the bad news, but he always boasted that he had prayed about it when good news was forthcoming.

Don't get me wrong, I am not trying to convince anyone that there is no God. I simply believe that traditional religions have been absolutely absurd in trying to describe and define "God."

Church Hymns

◇◇◇◇◇◇◇◇◇◇◇◇◇◇◇◇◇◇◇◇◇◇◇◇◇◇◇◇◇◇◇◇◇◇◇◇

MY COLLEGE ROOMMATE WAS convinced the persuasive music in church was the key to the bold conversions she had witnessed. "It's the music that does it to people," she claimed, and she is likely right. I try to forget that my father, the minister, laughed when I, a 10 year-old child, tearfully told him during my bold conversion, that the reason I knew I was "saved" is because I felt it. His laughter and prayer proved me wrong. He prayed, "Lord, we know we are saved, not because of a feeling, but because you have promised that if we believe in Jesus Christ, we will be saved." So, I was wrong at such an important crossroads in my life. But, that was very typical of my father. He laughed often, and very inappropriately – at others and at us. My sister claims that her inferiority complex was a direct result of my father laughing at her at certain times (after a curly perm, etc.) Mother warned him about it, but his reply was, "Oh, she doesn't need to be so sensitive." Maybe that was the impetus for my current philosophy to beware of feelings. Trust facts, not feelings and beliefs.

But, maybe my roommate was right. Perhaps it is "just the music." I can still see the modestly sized sanctuary decorated with silver chalices and burgundy carpet. I can still smell the communion wine (okay, grape juice since we were Baptists), and hear the droning and slurring of the powerful music, "Softly and Tenderly Jesus is Calling." That music was inviting enough to entice a cow to hold its head up and march proudly in for the slaughter. "Just as I am without one plea" was also compelling after I realized the word was "plea" instead of "flea."

Some of the words in the church hymns were foreign. What child knows what the word "sheaves" means? Therefore, when the congregation sang, "Bringing in the Sheaves," I automatically thought they were singing, "Bringing in the Sheets." I knew what that was because I had, after Mother's urgent demand to get the sheets on the clothesline in before a summer storm, frequently and frantically brought in the sheets.

One of my friends thought "Blessed Assurance" was "Blessed Insurance." Her father was an insurance salesman.

Since kids were completely bored in church – I mean, what child can sit quietly through a 30- minute sermon without getting restless? – we would make up quiet games to ease the boredom. We tried to be quiet, but sometimes we found things so funny, we were louder than intended. Nothing is more difficult than getting tickled in church and having to stifle the giggles.

One of the favorite quiet games was "Under the Sheets." We would look through the hymnal, and whatever the song title was, we would add (silently, of course), "under the sheets." Some of the best ones were:

Almost Persuaded

Bind Us Together

How Great Thou Art

I am Thine O Lord

I Have Decided to Follow Jesus

Jesus is Calling

Jesus Loves Me

Have Thine Own Way, Lord
Oh For a Thousand Tongues
Oh How I Love Jesus
Softly and Tenderly
Whiter Than Snow
There is a Fountain
There Shall be Showers of Blessing

My personal favorite was "Christ Arose."

I SEE CHRISTMAS

◇◇◇◇◇◇◇◇◇◇◇◇◇◇◇◇◇◇◇◇◇◇◇◇◇◇◇◇◇◇◇◇◇◇

WHEN MY MOTHER WOULD see any of our private parts, she would frequently say, in a very humorous and teasing tone, "I see Christmas." My partner thought that was hilarious and started using the term herself. After Mother died, my mother's best friend, Shelva, and I were sitting with Dad in the hospital. He had just had emergency surgery, so modesty was the farthest thing from his mind. As he struggled with the hospital gown and bed sheets, he became fully exposed. He either didn't care, or wasn't aware. I quipped, "I see Christmas." I explained to Shelva that Mother often used that expression when she saw one of us when we were nude. She commented that she had heard the expression used as well. We were talking about the origin of the expression – how anyone could equate nudity with Christmas, when Dad interrupted, "I don't mean to be nasty, but there are balls on Christmas trees."

PENNIES FROM HEAVEN

ONE OF MY MOTHER'S hobbies was looking for and picking up money she had found. She constantly and thoroughly scanned each setting for coins or cash. Her eyes were constantly searching under benches at malls, under tables in restaurants, in gas stations near pumps, and while standing in line at fast-food franchises. She frequently found money and was always elated when she did. Dad commented that one day she was going to get hit by a car or a truck while stopping in the middle of a road to pick up a penny. "The hospital bill would cost thousands," he argued, again making fun of her excitement about finding any stray coin on the street. One afternoon, she actually found $700.00 in bills in a fast-food restaurant. She told the manager she had found a large sum of money, and left her name and phone number with him in case anyone claimed a loss. No one did.

One day after Mother died, Dad and I were walking around his neighborhood. I stooped to pick up a penny. "What is the date on it?" Dad demanded. I told him I couldn't read it and asked why it mattered. "Because," he said, "I prayed that I would get a signal from your mother and she would leave me a penny with my birth year, 1925. You've heard about 'pennies from heaven' and that is what I prayed for."

On the way home, I thought it must be great to still believe in such magical thinking. Even if one believes in an afterlife, I would guess most people don't think the dead can actually manipulate tangible objects. On the drive back to my home, I realized that I could be responsible for answering that prayer. Was this divinely inspired? My partner just happens to be a coin collector. I told her of the plan and she willingly donated a 1925 penny. I placed it strategically so he would find it, and he was overjoyed. As someone explained one time, "The devil may have brought it, but God inspired it."

I, being a realist, had second thoughts, that this would reinforce others' beliefs that the dead have nothing better to do than hang around and send signs that they are still hovering. I knew Dad would tell everyone he saw. However, I thought if that is what will make him happy, I shall do this, and relish in the same joy for deception that he, Mother, and many parents do when they teach their children to believe in Santa, the tooth fairy, or the Easter Bunny. (Then they wonder why we are scared of being attacked by monsters at night and why we don't believe their assurances that nothing can get in the house to get us.)

Dad has always been extremely self-centered, and I was complaining to my partner that he should have prayed for a coin that bore Mother's year of birth, or their anniversary. But, of course, he wanted a coin with his birth year on it. I was very tempted to plant a 1929 coin anyway, to see if his story changed, but I just couldn't do it.

POST-DEATH DREAMS

◇◇◇◇◇◇◇◇◇◇◇◇◇◇◇◇◇◇◇◇◇◇◇◇◇◇◇◇◇◇◇◇◇◇◇◇◇◇

I HAD TWO VERY vivid dreams of my mother after she died. In the first one, the receptionist at work told me that I had a phone call. "And, Mara," she said with a very shaking voice, "It's your mother." Of course I thought it was a prank. I grabbed the phone and said, "Hello." "Mara," my mother began, "This is Mother" – as she had always started a phone conversation. I must have awakened, because I don't remember anything else about that conversation.

With my psychology background, I am intrigued by dreams and try to determine their source. I had not disclosed this to many people, but I did just mention to the receptionist that my father would hold Mother's picture and talk to her very often. He would usually say, "Hi Sweetie," and then proceed to tell her all that was going on that day. I mentioned to the receptionist that I had told Dad it wasn't silly if it made him feel better (although I do wish he would not tell the whole world he does this, or talk so loudly she probably can really hear him). The receptionist laughed and said, "As long as she doesn't talk back to him." So, I was sure that conversation was the impetus for the dream.

The second dream was more vague but our family was trying to decide who was going to perform a certain task. Mother was there and kept volunteering, but we all knew she couldn't really do it because she was no longer alive. She, however, did not seem to understand that she was incapable of contributing.

I had never experienced a death of a close family member before, so I did not know how I was going to react. I keep trying to tell myself that she was so sick, I was very glad she was no longer suffering. I keep convincing myself that I was very lucky to have 55 years of knowing her, most of those in great health, particularly since some people lose their mothers at very early ages. It's true, though, no matter what kind of relationship you have with your parents, you'll miss them when they are gone. I do wish that Mother and I could have had the opportunity to talk more and visit with each other more without my father's incessant self-absorbed chatter. But, maybe there will be other times for that – maybe not. All I know is, anything is better than the suffering and dependency she experienced in her last few days of life. I still cannot believe that anyone who witnesses someone in such pain and states of deterioration isn't an ardent proponent of euthanasia.

I know there are those who believe that everyone has a time to live and a time to die, and God decides when that will be. However, I just do not think a loving and just God would cause that much pain in anyone, particularly in children and the elderly.

Polar Opposites

HOW CAN TWO PEOPLE from the same gene pool not only have hardly anything in common, but be polar opposites? I was trying to determine what Dad was interested in doing since he seemed to show no interest in anything. He used to enjoy shopping but he can no longer stand for any period of time. I thought he might enjoy riding around in one of the electric carts. He claims he is afraid he will run into someone because his "mind is not good." (He always points to the side of his head when talking about his mind.) Besides, he doesn't even enjoy browsing anymore. I asked him what he liked to do the most, and he said the thing he enjoyed the most was going to church on Sunday. Let me just say that I would truly rather spend a whole day digging ditches than to go to an evangelical church for an hour. My least enjoyable activity on Sunday would involve getting dressed, going to church and sitting there while somebody insisted on trying to teach me something and yelled that we were all going to hell if we didn't repent. I can't imagine that anyone would find that enjoyable, but our differences make the world interesting.

Another extreme difference in our thinking involves our perception of food. Dad, as mentioned before, makes purchasing decisions based on cost, and does not appear to value quality as much. I, however, value quality. I would rather pay $2.00 for a good cup of coffee than have a free cup of coffee that tastes terrible. He thinks it is outrageous to pay more than 50 cents for coffee. I would rather pay $5.00 for a nutritious sandwich with fresh vegetables than to pay $1.00 for a pre-packaged artery-clogging "burger" at a fast food restaurant. When I buy coffee at Starbucks, he always says, "You must have plenty of money."

Dad also values beliefs and I value scientific facts. One day during lunch, I read on a bottle cap that bullfrogs do not sleep (although I later learned that this is not yet scientific fact). Dad said he didn't believe it. This man who believes the story of Noah's ark, who believes in death resurrected, who believes that beings exist who never were born or will never die, and believes in all kinds of miracles because that stuff is in the Bible, can't manage to believe that bullfrogs don't sleep.

Except for the aforementioned Easter bonnet, our taste in clothes has always been fairly aligned. One spring, however, my parents decided to give me a suit for my birthday. Mother made certain I knew that Dad picked it out for me. He typically has pretty good taste. For some reason, however, this loud, floral print suit caught his eye and he decided it was just the thing. I tried to be gracious when I opened it. I returned it the first chance I got.

When I entered the store in my typical androgynous garb and informed the clerk I wanted to return the suit because I just did not like it, she peered at me through her reading glasses for a few seconds, obviously saw that my typical apparel was more of a unisex style, looked at the suit, stared at me again, looked at the suit, and asked, "Somebody bought this for you?" I nodded. She declared, "Somebody's trying to change your image."

PULPIT GOOFS!

EVEN THOUGH MY FATHER was an English major and had a great grasp of grammar and an above average vocabulary, slang was not his strength. Mom used to warn him about using expressions that he didn't really understand. One Sunday, he was preaching and said, "And if you don't believe that brother, you are SOL." After church, a member asked him if he knew what the term meant. Dad admitted he didn't and confessed he was just using it as an expression. My father, who never used profanity in his life, was really embarrassed when he was informed that he had told the congregation they were "Shit out of luck." The church members were fanning themselves and their shoulders were shaking violently in their attempts to stifle their laughter. Perhaps his biggest pulpit goof, however, was when he was trying to say "The fiery darts of the wicked," and instead said, "The diry farts of the wicked." He continued while several who were actually paying attention to the sermon struggled to maintain their composure.

When my Dad was on vacation in Birmingham, Alabama, he started having extreme visual problems and was diagnosed with a detached retina. The post-surgery mandates required him to extend his stay. He called the head deacon of the church and explained that he would not be back as soon as expected because he had a detached retina, so a substitute minister would be required for Sunday services.

The deacon stood in the pulpit to inform the congregation of the news and said, "The preacher will not be with us today. He called and said he had to have surgery for a detached rectum."

That really sounds painful.

Angst – iety!

MY MOTHER WAS QUITE the anxious person. She did not realize it, however. As adults, when we were planning to go to the beach, she would warn us about all the things that could possibly happen. "Be sure to wear sunscreen, or you'll get skin cancer. Don't go in the water, you'll drown. Don't go in the water, something will bite you and you will be paralyzed for life." When I mentioned to her one day that she seemed unusually anxious and recommended that she talk with her physician about it, she responded very innocently, "I'm not anxious." When I referenced numerous examples of how her anxious behavior compared to a normal person's, she laughed. When referencing the statements above, I emphasized that most people would say to their children, "Have a nice time, Dear" and that was what we were hoping to hear. Instead, it was a barrage of cautions and warnings of what could happen.

How does one enjoy life being so anxious? I ask jokingly, because, unfortunately, I inherited a little of the anxiety. So, let me take you into an anxious person's mind for a few minutes. I wake up one morning with exceptionally bad breath. My first thought is I must have eaten something that disagreed with me. However, when my anxiety overtakes the internal conversation, it becomes, "It smells like decay – Oh God, my bowels must be rotting from some horrible disease." You see how quickly the anxious person thinks the worst? When a loved one is late, the normal person's thought is, "She must have had to work late." The anxious brain screams, "Oh God, she has been in an accident and is seriously hurt or dead."

While driving, many people fail to watch out for the other guy. I agonize over everyone I encounter. Is that person going to pull out in front of me? Is that person going to come over in my lane? Is this the day I get into a bad wreck and end up in the hospital with permanent brain damage? Is a deer going to jump out in front of me and cause me to wreck? As you can see, driving can be far from a pleasurable experience if the anxious brain dominates.

I can't imagine how, but, somehow I managed to score a little high on the anxiety test given to all college sophomore guinea pigs. As a result, I entered a study for relaxation training. It was one of the best things I have ever done. My sleepless nights, because I was sure that someone was going to break in the house each night, were replaced with restful, anxious-free slumber after I learned to concentrate specifically and exclusively on relaxing my body parts. The gun I bought for self-protection added another layer of confidence. Some of my right-leaning friends are surprised to know that I own a gun. But, after all, I do live in the South, and I consider a gun a great "equalizer." I love my 38 special and intend to keep it. But, I don't need a high-powered weapon to protect myself, my home and my loved ones, so I do believe in limiting gun access and insuring that people who own guns are mentally stable (background checks). I do not see a need for high-capacity ammunition because I do not anticipate that this earth will be invaded by aliens or more than one or two people will try to break into my house at a time. My 38 special will be sufficient.

With the tragedies we have experienced, particularly with the murder of countless, small, innocent children in Connecticut, it is beyond belief that our representatives did not feel the need to protect their citizens by getting these dangerous guns out of the hands of anyone but the military. It is hard for me to reconcile that the same individuals who are so ardently opposed to abortion can be such ardent supporters of high-capacity weapons that resulted in the massacre of numerous young children. I would hope that they would feel a greater need to protect live, breathing children than they do fetuses.

Another manifestation of the generalized anxiety I have involves the social realm. With the exception of an intimate dinner with my closest friends, I am one who would rather sit at home with a good book than attend a party. My social anxieties surface when I am invited to an event with people I do not know. I wonder if I will be able to think of things to talk about. A good conversationalist I am not.

While most people, when invited to a party, are excited about the prospect of an enjoyable time, I and other anxiety-prone individuals start the internal process that goes something like… Will people like me? Will I make a fool of myself? Will I do something to embarrass myself or someone else? Will I say something stupid or offensive? Will I be able to carry on an intelligent conversation and think of interesting things to say?

I have learned to manage my anxiety using self-talk in lieu of medication. I tell myself that I should not expect the worst, that I should enjoy the activity or event and control my anxiety by breathing.

PRAYER

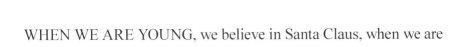

WHEN WE ARE YOUNG, we believe in Santa Claus, when we are teenagers, we don't believe in Santa Claus; when we adults, we ARE Santa Claus.

Many people have expressed the desire to pray for me. I am sure they believe I am going to hell if I don't change my ways. While I appreciate the underlying sentiment (I guess) that they wish to spend eternity with me, I am constantly amused by most bible-thumpers lack of biblical knowledge. Jesus himself, in Matthew 6:5-6 advises us to pray secretly – behind closed doors. So much for the movement to have public prayers.

I admire all religious people who understand that religion should be a private matter, and who live by example rather than intimidation or unsolicited influence. I am so disheartened by the extremist Christians, Muslims, etc. who seem hell-bent on forcing their religious values down other peoples' throats. I know they fervently believe that their "path" is the only genuine, authentic "road to salvation" but where did love for our fellowman (and woman) go? They seem to lack any respect for people of different faiths and beliefs.

Even some self-proclaimed atheists think that, although a huge bearded man in the sky does not exist, God exists in us all. The thinking is similar to the belief in Santa Claus. When we are young, we are taught that Santa Claus is real and he lives at the North Pole and makes toys for kids. When we are older and more able to understand that Santa makes lots of neat things for rich kids, but very little for poor kids – and something is not right here! Later, we are able to understand the "spirit" of Santa Claus and that, we, in fact, are all potential Santa Clauses because of our willingness to spread Christmas cheer. God, in some opinions, is identical. Although a being may not necessarily exist, that only obliges us to act God-like, help each other, love each other, and take care of each other as best as we humanly can do.

MIDDLE SCHOOL AND BEYOND

◇◇◇◇◇◇◇◇◇◇◇◇◇◇◇◇◇◇◇◇◇◇◇◇◇◇◇◇◇◇◇◇◇◇◇◇◇◇

MIDDLE SCHOOL IS CHALLENGING for most people, but particularly for those who are depleted of their self-confidence. I don't think there are any middle school students who are brimming with self-confidence, but I am talking about the painfully shy, very introverted group. One of my goals in life was to help people solve their problems. I always admired those girls who were sought-after counselors – those who seemed to really be able to help by listening and giving sound, nonjudgmental, common-sense advice. I never wanted to burden anyone with my own problems. I thought I was strong enough to handle whatever came my way by myself, but I knew there were those who really benefitted from sound advice from a trusted friend. When I was in 8th grade, I met a fantastic girl who later became my best friend. Margaret was her name, and everyone loved her. She was the nicest person who seemed to have the most common sense of anyone I had ever met. I was fortunate that our friendship flourished through the 9th grade. That is when my father decided he was going to leave to pastor another church in another town. I was devastated and angry. I couldn't believe he had been "called" to lead another church. I later discovered he knew he was called because the other church offered him a higher salary. God works in mysterious ways.

Margaret and I vowed to not let distance destroy our friendship. We did maintain a friendship via letters (e-mail or texting was a thing of the future), and decided we would both attend a nearby university and room together. We fulfilled that vow, and it was one of the best experiences of my life.

But, in middle school, I found out that "under the guise of leadership," I was becoming "dictatorial." Since I was only in 8th grade, I had to look up several words in the dictionary to find out what that meant, but my 8th grade teacher, who seemed to take an instant disliking to me, had reported that, in writing, to my parents. It actually appeared on my report card. Never mind that there was a boy in the class who told others what to do, too. He, however, had "excellent leadership skills" while I, a female, was "dictatorial." Upon further investigation, I found out that my 8th grade teacher had disliked my older sister, so she probably decided any kin of hers was not going to have an easy time in her classroom. I was falsely accused of cheating, and then thought, "If I am going to be accused of things, I may as well have the fun of actually doing them." So, I had a pretty fun 8th grade year by no longer caring about impressing my teachers. During the same year, my older sister just casually mentioned to me that I "talked too loudly" so I did nothing but mumble for the next few years.

Speaking of my older sister – she is, undoubtedly the one who contributed the most to my self-consciousness. She told me I had no rhythm, so I refused to dance for a very long time. She said she wished her breasts were as big as mine, so I started slouching in an attempt to minimize the effect. Maybe straight women can relate to this, but I have never met a dyke who wanted larger breasts. Of course, most people hear things like this during their lives but are not sensitive enough to allow these careless comments to change behavior so drastically. I, on the other hand would not readily admit anything but strength. In fact, I never admitted I was tired because I thought that was a sign of weakness. However, deep down, I was very sensitive, and sometimes very tired.

When I first moved to the new school that was out into the farthest reaches of the boondocks, I realized I hated my parents for making this change, and I hated my whole life for feeling so differently about things than my parents. I wanted cool parents, rich parents (who doesn't?), parents who understood how passionate I was about the people I admired, and really despised them for separating Margaret and me. I decided immediately that I would hate the new high school and everything in it. I realize a more mature decision would have been to "get with the program" or "go with the flow" but I was not mature – even for a mere 10th grader. I was so shy, one of my friends later told me that I looked as though if someone said "hello" I would start crying. In this small school, I was the "new girl" so I was under a magnifying glass. I was a pretty strong student, so I decided the only hope for me was to succeed academically for the next three years until I could get out of this hell-hole and on to college. So that is what I did. I did not get involved in any extra-curricular activities unless forced. (Everyone had to be in a club since the members met during school hours.) Fortunately, the school had some very good teachers, so my decision to just survive academically was a good one after all.

Ms. Pruitt was the teacher I admired greatly. Okay, I'll admit, I had a huge crush on her. I started signing up for all the math courses, and would work hours on math assignments to try to impress her. My mother wanted me to be an accountant since my math scores were so high, but accounting didn't really interest me. It wasn't the course work – it was Ms. Pruitt that was the motivation. She was this cute, little, southern talking woman who obviously (based on her breath when she leaned in to help us or check our work) smoked cigarettes and drank coffee during her breaks in the teachers' lounge. Her husband was a tobacco farmer so she sported a huge bumper sticker on her car that said, "Enjoy smoking" during the beginning of the tobacco controversy. I survived high school thanks to a really great friend, Jacque, and a pretty neat guy I dated who I later found out was gay.

I changed dramatically in college. I was searching for myself, and my journey took me through some quite dangerous but very memorable encounters. I wouldn't change a thing about my past experiences (on second thought, maybe a few). There was nothing I enjoyed more than an intimate philosophical conversation with a brilliant person. Jacque ended up transferring to the same college, so we continued our friendship and our enlightening conversations. She was a Mormon, and was the first person I met who didn't believe in hell. "How could I go to hell" she argued, "when it doesn't exist?" Jacque was one of my most intelligent friends, and I was so honored that she would even want to talk to me, much less be my friend. We had some great experiences together, and I will cherish them for a lifetime.

CRUSHES

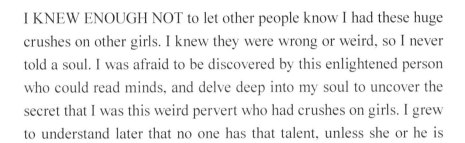

I KNEW ENOUGH NOT to let other people know I had these huge crushes on other girls. I knew they were wrong or weird, so I never told a soul. I was afraid to be discovered by this enlightened person who could read minds, and delve deep into my soul to uncover the secret that I was this weird pervert who had crushes on girls. I grew to understand later that no one has that talent, unless she or he is really good with a Rorschach.

Mother may have suspected something early on. I remember being told by her one Sunday evening, "You are too old to be holding hands with Barbara Dixon." I was crushed. Barbara and I were buddies. We loved playing Cowboys and Indians. She let me tie her up.

The first crush I can ever remember, however, was on a family friend named Linda. I was about 5 years old. She would baby-sit for us on occasion, and she was such fun to be around. She played cowboys with us and her back became the horse. She would crawl around on the floor while we, the cowgirls, rode her. She would try to gently buck us off. I think she was about the first person I ever personally knew who was homosexual.

My next big crush was in the 7th or 8th grade and was on a basketball coach named Carolyn. Nobody would describe her as attractive. She had crossed eyes, shortly cropped hair, and slurred speech. I, however, thought she was the bomb, and would ride my bicycle miles just to ride by her house. (Okay, so I was a bit of a stalker.) A couple of times, I decided a car would get me there faster, so I drove my father's car to that neighborhood while he was in the shower. When my Dad went into the bathroom, he was consistently there for at least one hour. So, I would go driving. I did mention that I was in the 7th or 8th grade and was much too young for a license. I still appreciate my younger sister for not ever telling.

The pattern had been established. I had never experienced these crushes on boys or men. My sisters would talk dreamily about these movie or rock stars, and I just wouldn't see it. I did, however, love Julie Andrews and Carole King. I thought my sisters were silly for getting so nervous before dates that they would actually throw up. Although I never threw up, I did realize the anxiety that accompanies "wanting to impress." I never was anxious when dating boys, however.

Life seemed to be richer when I had a "crush" so I typically could name someone (not aloud though) I was attracted to during a certain time. After Margaret, came Leslie.

My attraction to her was so intense, the whole denial venture hit me square in the face. Leslie was straight and it killed me that her ugly boyfriend was allowed to kiss and hold her when I could not.

My next crush was on Molly. She was a sweet and intelligent nursing student who had the hots for Charlie. Again, there was no way he was good enough for Molly. He wasn't smart enough, good-looking enough, nice enough or rich enough. Again, I experienced extreme jealousy since there were seemingly no boundaries for their attraction, but I couldn't even verbalize mine – to anyone.

Thankfully, I survived my high school and college years with only minimal scars, most likely because I remained closeted. Some of the counseling groups for gays try to stress that life gets better, and it really is true. Life is much better as a gay adult than it is as a middle or high school student. We all need to be much more supportive of our gay brothers and sisters, and try to help them stay sane enough - alive even - to make that transition into adulthood.

KILL 'EM WITH KINDNESS

ACCORDING TO THE CATHOLIC Priest at the funeral of one of my co-workers, Mother Teresa said three things were important: kindness, kindness, and kindness. I sadly realized that kindness was the main ingredient missing in our household. Dad called Mother "Dumb Dora" every chance he got. I guess he thought that made him feel and appear smarter. She finally put her foot down and convinced him that it would not be good for his daughters to hear him being so critical of her. He also never overlooked a chance to remind her that he thought her older sister, Dorcas, was the prettiest girl in her family. His major form of entertainment seemed to be making fun of people, whether it was us, our neighbors, or the church members. Not that Mother was much kinder. She would say some pretty nasty things to us when she was irritated, and I now realize that since she was around Dad so much, she was always irritated. He would get himself ready on Sunday morning, go out to the car, get in the car and start blowing the horn. All she had to do was get herself and us three girls ready. She finally convinced him that blowing the horn when she was desperately trying to get ready was not good for his health, so that behavior ceased.

As I was older, I tried to have compassion for my father, but it is very difficult. He is a cantankerous old man who complains incessantly that the Mexicans and Blacks are taking over the United States. He watches *FOX News* continuously and swears that it is "fair and balanced." I understand people wanting a conservative alternative, but it is those people who think *FOX News* is true news, instead of a conservative commentary on the news, that concern me. I know *The Daily Show* and *MSNBC* are liberally slanted, and although I am a huge fan of *The Daily Show* and the *Colbert Report*, I am smart enough to realize that they are commentaries with a liberal bias – not the real news.

My father can't hear anymore, and although he spent over five thousand dollars for hearing aids (he calls them ear plugs), he refuses to wear them most of the time. I can tell immediately when he is wearing them. He talks in a normal tone. If he is not wearing them, he yells. I have told him many times not to yell at me because I can hear just fine, but he is very self-centered so he believes that if he can't hear, no one else can either. Trying to talk to him is exasperating. Ninety-nine percent of the time after something is said, his response is, "Huh?" Things have to be repeated several times before he can hear them. He does this even when he is wearing his hearing aids. I think it is either just an annoying habit, or he has some kind of auditory processing disorder and is stalling to allow time for him to process adequately. Most of the time, however, it is probably that he just can't hear, because he refuses to wear his hearing aids.

So, in his small house, he has the television turned to the highest volume, and it is deafening. Complaints to turn it down are countered with protests of "I can't hear it." Therefore, the only thing I can do to maintain my sanity in his house is to do like Mother did all those years – find something outside to do. But, you can still hear FOX news from any place in the yard (or neighborhood).

Loud noises are torturous to me. One thing I do not like about summer, besides the numerous people who are under-clothed, is the obnoxious rattle screaming from distorted, malfunctioning speakers whose owner obviously thinks it is cool to expose everyone to the sickening, writhing base emanating from his vehicle. I could withstand physical torture better than torture through excessive noise. I don't think anyone would have to even begin to send loud noises my way. All it would take is the threat of interrupting the solitude and quiet I cherish. I would tell all.

I try to be patient, but have little patience with someone who is very self-centered and will not budge or has never shown any consideration for others. However, I think Mother Teresa was right. If we could all just be kind to each other, what a great place the world would be. I agree with her, I can't imagine anything of more importance. My psychology training has taught me that we can never truly change anyone else. We may be able to change a few behaviors, but not basic personalities. We can only change ourselves, so I will have to try to be kinder and more patient.

CHRISTMAS FROM HELL

OF HIS THREE DAUGHTERS, I live closest to my father, even though it takes two hours and 45 minutes - no matter how you go to reach his house. I think I have tried 60 different ways in attempts to shave off a few minutes, but the shortest time is always 2 hours and 45 minutes. Because I am the closest, he spends Christmas at my house. This particular Christmas, my partner and I had decided to travel on to Charleston, South Carolina after we took him back home the day after Christmas. However, we had not heard about the approaching snow storm.

The snow started in the afternoon of Christmas Day and lasted through the next day. We did not get a huge amount of snow, but in Northeastern North Carolina, things close when two inches fall. Our governmental officials do not have the equipment to deal with the foot of snow that blanketed the area and brought everything to a standstill. Main roads are plowed but not secondary roads. We happen to live on a secondary road. We shoveled the driveway vigorously. Snow blew back into the driveway about an hour later, so it was impossible to even tell that we had shoveled it in the first place. We shoveled again. Nobody was more motivated than I to take Dad back home, so I shoveled with great abandon. Again, the snow blew back to cover the driveway. Our neighbor reported that their son had tried to get to town, and he had landed in a ditch. We were stuck.

My father's greatest joy, besides church, is going out to eat and he feels compelled to eat out every day. If he cannot, he is not happy. When he is not happy, no one around him is happy. He wanted to go out to eat lunch the day after Christmas. After all, he did not go anywhere on Christmas Day and I do not think he has had a time in his adult life where he was unable to go out to eat two days in a row. I told him we could not get out of the driveway. He was very distressed, but I doubt he was any more distressed than we were since it was becoming more apparent that our pre-paid vacation was going to be a total loss – not to mention that I would be house-bound with my father for a few more days.

He started complaining about his thumb. He has told us before that he likes sympathy. I do not like whiners. My partner was a little sympathetic. He said he needed to go to the doctor. I suspected another motive. He asked if I could call a cab.

Hold on!!!! Dad's incessant complaining about not being able to go anywhere anymore because he couldn't drive was met with arguments that he could call a cab and go anywhere he wanted in Goldsboro. His immediate scowl and head shaking was followed by a booming declaration, "I am not going to take a cab." He never gave a reason for his aversion to cabs, just insisted he was not going to call a cab.

So, this plea for a cab was very serious. Was he in that much pain? Was he that manipulative? I wasn't sure about the first, but he was definitely that manipulative. I explained that if we couldn't get out, a cab couldn't get in. When my partner finally babied him and gave him adequate attention for his hurting thumb, he calmed down.

My sister was planning to visit Dad after Christmas at his house. She lives in Pennsylvania and has an SUV. I called her. "You have got to come get him. He is driving me crazy," I pleaded. She laughed!

After a few more days of shoveling, we finally managed to get him home but were unable to be compensated for the pre-paid vacation since we did not bother to get insurance. Since it was December, we assumed we would not have any adverse weather conditions. Hurricanes are expected in the fall, but snowstorms of that magnitude are almost unheard of here.

LIBERAL VS. CONSERVATIVE

◇◇◇◇◇◇◇◇◇◇◇◇◇◇◇◇◇◇◇◇◇◇◇◇◇◇◇◇◇◇◇◇◇

MY MOTHER LEFT A book she had written that conveyed her thoughts about her daughters. This book was kind of a biographical documentary of my life – the birth statistics, her emotions when seeing me for the first time, a record of major developmental milestones, childhood memories, etc. One thing my mother said was that she hoped I married one of my childhood friends, a male of course, when I grew up. This was **after** she knew I was gay. I thought it was so sad, and felt so slighted. I was wondering why she just couldn't say, "I hope you are happy."

In the book, Mother also mentioned that I was a liberal and she was conservative. Recently, scientists have attempted to determine whether the brains of liberals and conservatives differ. On the MSN news Website on Saturday, March 2, 2013, Mandy Oaklander of Prevention magazine reported that brain scans could reliably reveal a person's political affiliation. The results of the study showed that when confronted with risky situations, gray matter in Democrats showed more activation in the left posterior insula, the region linked with empathy and emotion. The right amygdala was activated in the Republican brains, however. That region is associated with fear, reward, and a fight-or-flight response.

I would much rather have an empathic brain than one that is fearful and is constantly in a state of "fight or flight." Perhaps that explains why my parents are so "fearful" that the Blacks and Mexicans are "taking over everything" and I don't share those fears. Perhaps that explains why I am able to enjoy walks outdoors and can focus on the beauty of the surroundings while Mother always focused on those "aggravating dandelions." Perhaps that explains why Dad cannot enjoy the beauty of state parks because the descriptions of how certain things were formed, and how old certain things are in direct contrast to his beliefs about creation. Give me the liberal brain any time!

EXCURSION – RETURN TO YONDER

◇◇

ONE OF MY GOOD friends had a sister who died after a painfully lengthy illness. My friend stayed with her sister almost constantly throughout that difficult time, and provided daily reports of her experiences with her sister. She was elated when her sister could communicate with them, laugh, enjoy the sunset and the breeze on her face, and reminisce about their childhood days.

Five of us, including our friend's partner, attended the funeral to provide support for our friend. These things are always uncomfortable for us - we, lesbians, romping into a Baptist church where we are looked upon with disgust by many of the Christians. Sure, some of them try very hard to be friendly with us, but the looks we get when they think no one is watching…. At least, it seems acceptable now to wear slacks to church. First, when the minister was talking about the deceased person's family, he mentioned her older sister, a straight woman, and her husband. Though my friend had been by her sister's side for much of the year-long illness, the minister did not mention her. After the funeral the speculation was that he did not know how or what to say about the partner who was seated with her, and probably did not even have the slightest inclination to bring it up.

Did I mention it was a Baptist church? So, one of the songs was "When the Roll is Called up Yonder." Now, 30 years ago, I had no idea how funny the words to this song were. I now have a tremendous appreciation for it. This song is just plain hilarious. While I was thinking about how humorous the words were, I turned to my Catholic friend, intending to say, "I bet you have never heard this song." The bemused expression on her face was one of the funniest things I have seen. You know, everything is much funnier in church.

During the service, the minister spoke of the deceased husband's love. He said, "All women want is a man to love them." We four lesbians on the back row were flabbergasted. It was utterly amazing to go back in time (to the 15th century it seemed) and be told that we want a man to love us. Our Jewish friend also had some things to say about the minister's attempt to save her, and everyone else in the congregation during a funeral service, no less.

That was my world for 20 years, but I am so glad it no longer is. And in the rural South, it is very difficult for us to navigate our way into these social events. The sister's partner said she was tired of all the derisive looks she received from the church members. While her coping mechanism was one of retreat, mine is more upfront. I have never been one to throw my sexuality in anyone's face, but I am certainly not going to retreat in the face of bigotry and hatred anymore. I will proudly declare my partnership with the most loving person on the earth. In fact, I think I will start describing her as my fiancée, because we most certainly have agreed to marry – first chance we get. Albeit, it probably won't be in that church!

Book Gone Bad

◇◇◇◇◇◇◇◇◇◇◇◇◇◇◇◇◇◇◇◇◇◇◇◇◇◇◇◇◇◇◇◇◇◇◇◇

MY FIRST BOOK VENTURE did not turn out exactly as I had hoped. My goal for that book was to reference the strangest verses in the Bible. I knew there were some very weird verses, but had no idea how many until I had read the entire Bible and recorded what I thought were the strangest verses. Frankly, I did not want to include a lot of commentary – I wanted the Bible verses to speak for themselves, and I wanted the book to serve as a reference for those interested in searching strange verses referencing women, children, demons, etc. Unfortunately, the world of publishing does not think that way. It seems that 80 percent has to be original work. So, after 104 pages of work, I hit a brick wall. The publisher called it a "glitch." I called it a major barrier – and a deal breaker. I finally decided that I could incorporate the major findings into this book, and still provide the reader with a basic knowledge of the weirdest Bible verses. My goal was to give myself, and hopefully, any readers, education about the Bible, and ammunition that may be needed for future Biblical or political arguments. The forward of this now elusive work follows:

FORWARD FOR THE BOOK GONE BAD

◇◇◇

IS THE BIBLE GOD'S "Holy Word?" Were the Bible's authors so divinely inspired that the teachings are infallible? Some people's religious convictions are based on the belief that the Bible is God's holy word. "The Scriptures" are used to defend various political principles and moral judgments. Quotes from both the Old and New Testaments are used to vehemently castigate those who would be so defiant as to defend abortion and homosexuality, while other references in identical books of the Bible that clearly state adulterers should be put to death, are ignored.

I knew when I was young that something was not right with the religious brainwashing I experienced. How does one reconcile being a girl or a woman, much less a lesbian, with the teachings of the church? We had no female ministers, deacons, not even female ushers. How could I and all the other females truly believe that we could be anything we wanted – scientists, engineers, doctors – when we could not even be an usher in our own church? Even though my father and certainly not my mother did not overtly discourage us (although I do recall hearing my father say girls couldn't do or be certain things) we would have had to have been blind and deaf not to recognize the abounding sexism and prejudices. During the 50's and 60's the most important function of the deacons seemed to be to insure that no black people entered our church doors. That seems to defy all the Christian teachings – or does it?

Have you ever really read the entire Bible? I could not say that I had. I went to church, it seems, my entire child life. We had services on Sunday mornings, Sunday evening, and Wednesday evenings. We had Sunday School, League, Vacation Bible School - (the week right after school was out for the summer – which I considered the cruelest of all timing); and revival twice per year that meant church every single night of the week. So, of course, I had read and heard many select passages, but had never sat down and read the entire thing. For one thing, it's LONG, and the print is very small. But my father, the minister, served as the motivation for me to read the entire manuscript. After my mother died, he had decided he was going to read the entire thing – front to back - for the second time in his life. Periodically, he would ask me if I had ever heard of certain passages, and said he did not know that was in the Bible. For example, he asked if I knew that the Bible said adulterers should be put to death (Leviticus 20:10). Specifically, it says, "And the man that committeth adultery with another man's wife, even he that committeth adultery with his neighbor's wife, the adulterer and the adulteress shall surely be put to death." I did not, in fact, know of that verse, but thought, "If this man, who spent his entire life studying and teaching the Bible, is surprised about its contents, what is really in there?" So, I decided to find out.

Once I began reading it, I realized that it is very scary, depressing, redundant and boring. Genesis starts out with a bang – recounting murders and rapes. God's "orders" for the appropriate way to construct a temple and an altar are pages and pages of seemingly obsessive specifications. God is described as loving and kind, yet "He" murders little children, babies, etc. because their relatives do not comply with his wishes. Reading the Bible is faith-shaking to the most ardent believers and I realized I was quickly losing any possible tiny remnant of religion I had left.

When one reconciles scientific teachings, common sense and natural observations, suddenly everything makes sense and we wonder why that insight was not apparent earlier. I had experimented with Episcopalianism, Buddhism, and finally realized that I didn't need or frankly want an "organized" religion. That, in fact, I was not religious at all. Unfortunately, there is no turning back. Once that point is reached, everything suddenly makes sense.

Please understand that I am neither defending nor denouncing spirituality, religion or atheism. Although there are many atheists, and their numbers that include former clergymen and women continue to grow, I would not try to convince others that atheism is the most appealing religious, or non-religious option. One can be spiritual without being religious, and can believe that "God" can be found in almost every living thing and experience. Therefore, one can believe in the "spirit" of God without believing in God himself. Most certainly, I am not a biblical scholar and have never claimed to be. I'm sure there will be criticism that some of the commentary is unfair because the verses are quoted without a contextual reference. Therefore, I urge the reader to review the preceding and subsequent verses to determine the particular context.

Religion certainly has had and continues to have a great influence on our culture. I have heard and believe that people with religious ties are generally happier than those without. Affiliation with a church can provide a strong sense of community and very positive experiences. The church provides much comfort and support to people, and some people are in need of a "tribe" that the church family can provide. I am merely cautioning against the use of fundamental teachings to guide our legislation. I am advocating for an understanding of the positive elements of religious teachings (treating others kindly). If we lived by that alone, what a great place the world would be.

One only has to observe the faces of people during religious experiences to see that religion provides a sense of pleasure – perhaps even endorphin release – that people seek. Others may find the same pleasure in music, nature, helping others, and drugs. If people abide by the 10% tithing directive, the amount of money contributed to a church can be financially draining to the donors, so participation in a particular church can be one of the most expensive ways to capture that ecstasy that many seek. But, can anyone invest too much in a future that includes the promise of everlasting life?

To remember that other people hold diametrically opposite but just as fervent beliefs is important. One of my colleagues spent quite a bit of time trying to convince me that her Sabbath, which her church celebrates on Saturday, was the correct one and everyone else was wrong in celebrating on Sunday. Does God really care which day is observed? Some fundamentalists Christians think Jews, Muslims, and Buddhists are wrong (going to hell even). Extremist Muslims think Christians are wrong. These steadfast, iron-clad beliefs are perceived as ridiculous by the people who hold the opposing view. Obviously, there are a lot of "wrong" people. Similarly, there are those that hold that evolution is non-existent because it contradicts the teachings of the church. Certainly, mistakes have been made in the name of science, but the evidence of evolution is incontrovertible. Perhaps those that deny evolution have not experienced it themselves?

Certainly, churches have their challenges. Filled with external and internal political influences, churches strive to maintain their status in the community and small churches struggle to avoid being consumed by mega-churches. Paul advises that church members work to get along so the church would not be split. We probably can't even begin to count the number of times the church has split because of fundamental differences. My father indicated that the "Nationals" – a term he uses disparagingly – split from his denomination when Mount Olive College, a college supported by his denomination, was established. The "Nationals" refused to support it because it was going to provide a "Liberal Arts" education and they didn't like the "liberal" terminology. I think the Amish are about the only people who are more conservative than my father, so this is most amusing to me.

My goal with this research was simply to encourage people to think independently. So many times we blindly adhere to the teachings of one philosophy that we fail to not only think for ourselves, but to open our minds to the ideas of others. Another goal, admittedly, is to provide an arsenal for those who so often are in the position of defending themselves from the vitriolic diatribes of the fundamentalists of any religion.

What we need is another period of enlightenment, because some people just didn't get the first one!

THE MOST BIZARRE BIBLE VERSES

SOME OF THE VERSES in the Bible are hilarious, others disturbing, and others just plain weird. Leviticus 13:45 commands lepers to rip their clothes and cry that they are unclean. Can you imagine someone running in the streets crying, "I am unclean," or "I am a leper"? In Leviticus 26, God threatens to make people eat their own sons and daughters. Dove's dung was sold in 2 Kings 6:25. That same chapter describes a woman who is distraught because another woman proposed an agreement with her to eat each other's children. However, after the distraught woman's child was eaten, the woman who had proposed the agreement hid her child so it could not be eaten.

2 Kings 18:27 says, *But Rabshakeh said unto them, Hath my master sent me to thy master, and to thee, to speak these words? hath he not sent me to the men which sit on the way, that they may eat their own dung, and drink their own piss with you?*

In Numbers, even an animal is given the power to speak. In Chapter 22 a man is beating his donkey, and the donkey asks the man why he is beating her.

The Old Testament contains references to numerous rapes, murders, wars, plagues, and obliterations. After all the very violent stories recounted in the first few chapters of the Bible, I was anxious to start reading the Psalms in anticipation of a more uplifting perspective. I remember reading the verse about "The Lord is my Shepherd, I shall not want...," so I was eager to find something, anything that would change the warped impression I had after reading the horrific events that unfolded in the previous chapters. So, my thought, when I reached the Psalms in the Bible was, "Thank goodness, finally some positive verses." I was really wrong. Perhaps the most disturbing verse in the entire Bible was found in Psalms 137:9 which says, "Happy shall he be, that taketh and dasheth thy little ones against the stones." When I share this verse with others, I am asked, "What is the context?" I think, "How can anyone in their right minds condone smashing little children or babies against rocks? There is no justification anywhere for that."

Other weird verses include the one in Chapter 6 of I Corinthians that says saints or Christians will judge the very angels in heaven, and Hebrews 7:3 that describes a being named Melchisedec who had no father or mother, was never born and will never die.

Most everyone knows that slavery is in the Bible. But, I was surprised to find how slaves are to be treated, based on Biblical teachings. In Exodus 21:20-21, the Bible says if a slave is beaten and he dies, the owner should be punished. However, if the slave lives for a few days before he dies, the owner should not be punished. So, slaves can be beaten within an inch of their lives, but as long as they live, that is acceptable. Lest we think that slavery is just an Old Testament proclamation, Colossians 3:22, which is in the New Testament, demands that servants obey their masters.

References to demons were particularly interesting. I remember as a teenager being terrified while watching the Exorcist. As an adult, however, I thought how ridiculous it was that I was so shaken by that movie. However, there are numerous references to demon possession in the Bible, so it must be true, right? In Matthew 17, Jesus' disciples were unable to cast one particular demon out of a boy, even though they claimed to have the requisite faith. But Jesus told them that particular demon would not leave until the disciples prayed and fasted. But the scariest verse about demons or spirits is found in Luke 11:24-26. Evidently when a demon is cast out, he goes to the deserts seeking rest. But when he finds none, he returns to the person he left taking seven other demons with him, and they all enter the man leaving him in a much worse state. So, I guess people who have demons invade their bodies are just SOL, as my father would say.

Another remarkable story about the persistence of demons is found in Acts 19:13-16. In this story, several Jews tried to cast demons out of a man by invoking the name of Jesus. The demon answered, "Jesus I know, and Paul I know but who are ye?" The demon then beat them, and the naked and wounded men fled.

THE STRANGEST BIBLE VERSES
ABOUT WOMEN AND CHILDREN

◇◇◇◇◇◇◇◇◇◇◇◇◇◇◇◇◇◇◇◇◇◇◇◇◇◇◇◇◇◇◇◇◇◇

WE ARE SO FORTUNATE that we did not live in Biblical times. As is evidenced by the following verses, women were viewed as property and by God's and Paul's command, were subservient to men. It seems the pain of childbirth and the curse of subservience was God's punishment for Eve's partaking of the apple (Genesis 3:16).

Numerous references to rape appear in the Bible. Deuteronomy 22:28-29 has been interpreted to mean that if a man rapes a girl, he must marry her and may never divorce her. How great is that for the girl? She is doomed to live with a rapist the rest of her life? Similarly, Judges 19:22-28 recounts a story of men trying to have sexual relations with a man who was a guest in a house. The master of the house offered his virgin daughter and the man's concubine, instead, and told the men to do with them as they wanted. The concubine was abused all night and ended up dying. So, it is better to rape and kill a woman than to have sexual relations with a man.

In Samuel 13:11-16, the story is told of Tamar who was raped by Amnon who later rejected her. Tamar said the rejection was worse than the rape. Furthermore, when her brother, Absalom, found out about the rape, he said, "Hold now thy peace, my sister: he is thy brother; regard not this thing." So, it is not so bad to be raped by a relative.

One of the strangest verses about women was found in Deuteronomy 25:11-12 that says: *When men strive together one with another, and the wife of the one draweth near for to deliver her husband out of the hand of him that smiteth him, and putteth forth her hand, and taketh him by the secrets: Then thou shalt cut off her hand, thine eye shall not pity her.* The "secrets" translates into testicles, meaning that if the woman is trying to help her husband in a fight by grabbing the other man's testicles, her hand should be cut off. This always reminds me of the time I was in first grade and helped one of my friends who was in a fight (and was losing). I jumped on the other boy. My father saw the whole thing and said, "If I ever find you fighting on that playground, I will blister your butt so badly you won't be able to sit down for days." At least I still have my arms. Of course, then again, I wasn't grabbing anyone's testicles.

Another Biblical directive that forces a no-win situation for women is found in Deuteronomy 22. If a man marries a woman who turns out not to be virgin he may divorce her, and the woman should be stoned to death. However, if he is wrong, he has to stay married to her, and may never divorce her. Evidently some kind of cloth had to be presented to the judges for this to be decided. I am assuming the cloth would contain the bloody evidence that the hymen had been broken by her first intercourse. Can you imagine the newly wedded couple carefully placing a cloth beneath them as they approach their post-wedding duties so they can be assured the women is a virgin? But, think about this, if she is not a virgin, she is stoned to death. If she is a virgin, she is forced to live with this jerk who has falsely accused her for the rest of her life. In the Bible, the women never win.

If men suspected their wives were unfaithful, they would bring the wife to a judge. She would have to drink bitter water. If she were unfaithful, the bitter water would make her thigh rot away and her body swell. Refer to Numbers 5 for the entire description. Perhaps this was the motivation for the bizarre Salem Witch Trials.

Biblical authors were certainly prejudiced against cranky women, too. Proverbs 21:19 says, "It is better to dwell in the wilderness, than with a contentious and an angry woman." Similarly, Proverbs 25:24 says, "It is better to dwell in the corner of the housetop, than with a brawling woman and in a wide house." Proverbs 27:15 reads, "A continual dropping on a very rainy day and a contentious woman are alike." No such verses regarding men were mentioned. I guess it is okay to be a cantankerous, grumpy man. My father is safe.

Women are depicted as having no wisdom (okay, as being stupid) in the Bible. In Ecclesiastes 7, a preacher is trying to count the number of wise people. One tenth of one percent of men was found to be wise, but not one woman. Maybe because we are stupid, we are supposed to be silent in church meetings. 1 Corinthians 14:34-35, and 1 Timothy 2:12 command that women remain silent in church meetings. Women are directed to ask their husbands if they have any questions about the meetings. But they have to wait until they return home to do so, because speaking in church is not allowed. Women also must obey their husbands (Ephesians 5:33; Titus 2:5) and submit to their husbands (Ephesians 5:22; Colossians 3:18).

Menstruating women seem to be particularly unclean. Leviticus 15:19 states, "And if a woman have an issue, and her issue in her flesh be blood, she shall be put apart seven days: and whosoever toucheth her shall be unclean until the even."

Children and animals are not spared from Biblical wrath. In 1 Samuel 15:3 and 1 Samuel 22:19, and Judges 20:48, men, women, children, babies, oxen, donkeys, sheep, and camels are destroyed. In

Chapter 15 of Judges, Samson sets the tails of foxes on fire to burn the fields. Horses are lamed in 2 Samuel, Chapter 8. Truly bizarre are the references to children being eaten (Deuteronomy 28:53; Deuteronomy 28:56-57; Lamentations 4:10). There are numerous other references to children and animals being killed in the Bible. I was very surprised and disgusted by all the references to killing innocent people, and there seemed to be little or no remorse for the random murder of young children and babies.

In the 2012 elections, Billy Graham placed full page ads in newspapers in North Carolina asking that people vote Biblical values. I ask you, what values? The ones that say it is okay to rape women, own slaves and beat them within an inch of their lives, torture animals and smash babies against rocks?

CONTRADICTIONS IN THE BIBLE

◇◇◇◇◇◇◇◇◇◇◇◇◇◇◇◇◇◇◇◇◇◇◇◇◇◇◇◇◇◇◇◇◇◇◇◇◇

DURING MY RESEARCH AND recordings of the strangest verses in the Bible, I discovered numerous contradictions and erroneous statements in the Bible. The first very obvious one was found in Genesis 1:14 that reads: "And God made two great lights; the greater light to rule the day, and the lesser light to rule the night." When the Bible was written, the moon was thought to be a light, but now we know this is not the case. I ask, however, if the Bible is the word of God, wouldn't the writers have been inspired to get it right?

The Bible has many versus that warn against eating certain things. Chapter 11 of Leviticus is very detailed and specific about which animals should not be eaten. Only fish with scales **and** fins, and animals that chew the cud **and** have cloven hooves should be eaten. Sea creatures without scales and fins (oyster, crabs, shrimp) and animals that either chew the cud or have cloven hooves (but not both) should not be eaten. Certain animals that crawl on the ground (mole, rat, snake, lizard) should also not be eaten. Leviticus 7:25-26 tells us that eating the blood and fat of animals is strictly prohibited. However, in Matthew 15:11, Jesus said, "Not that which goeth into the mouth defileth a man...." He further explains in Matthew 15:17, "Do not ye yet understand that whatsoever entereth in at the mouth goeth into the belly, and is cast out into the draught?" And Colossians

2:16 says, "Let no man therefore judge you in meat, or in drink, or in respect of an holyday, or of the new moon, or of the Sabbath days." So, I guess we can eat what we want after all. Not so fast! James 2:10 tell us, "For whosoever shall keep the whole law, and yet offend in one point, he is guilty of all."

Chapter 18 of Ezekiel and 2 Kings 14:5-7 firmly state that others should not pay for another's sins. Each person who sins is responsible for their own punishment. However, in Genesis 20:18, women are stricken with barrenness to punish someone else. In 1 Kings 21:28-29, Ahab's descendants are destroyed for his wrongdoings. In 2 Kings 5:27, a man's children (and his children's children) are cursed with leprosy. In Isaiah 65:6-7, payback is promised to men for the sins of their fathers.

Another contradiction involves God changing his mind. In Numbers 23:19-20, God is described as not being repentant or prone to reversing his decisions. However, 2 Samuel 24:16 and 1 Chronicles 21:15 describe God's changing his mind about the punishment he was executing.

Under the Law of Moses, men could be rid of their wives by writing a letter asking that she be dismissed. Jesus altered that law by stating, "…whosoever shall put away his wife, saving for the cause of fornication, causeth her to commit adultery; and whosoever shall marry her that is divorced committeth adultery." We find in Leviticus 20:10 that adultery is punishable by death. Chapter 2 of Colossians explains that certain rules were only temporary and ended when Christ came, and in Acts 15:27-29, only certain Jewish laws were said to be important.

Jesus was even contradictory about his own approach and reason for "being." In a commonly quoted passage, Matthew 11:28-30, Jesus states, "Come unto me, all ye that labor and are heavy laden, and I will give you rest. Take my yoke upon you, and learn of me; for I am meek and lowly in heart; and ye shall find rest unto your souls. For my yoke is easy, and my burden is light." Earlier, however, in Matthew 10:34, he says, "Think not that I am come to send peace on earth; I came not to send peace, but a sword." That doesn't sound "meek and lowly in heart" to me.

Exodus 31:15 warns, "Whosoever doeth any work in the sabbath day, he shall surely be put to death." But when some of the religious leaders were telling Jesus that some men should not be harvesting grains on the sabbath, Jesus replied, "The sabbath was made for man, and not man for the sabbath; therefore the Son of man is Lord also of the sabbath" (Mark 2:27-28).

In 1 Samuel 16:7, the Lord is telling Samuel that he doesn't make judgments about people based on outward appearances, but by their thoughts and intentions. But in the 21st chapter of Leviticus, men who are blind, lame, or have any defects are not permitted to offer sacrifices to the Lord. Also, Deuteronomy 23:1-2 states, "He that is wounded in the stones (testicles), or has his privy member cut off, shall not enter into the congregation of the Lord. A bastard shall not enter into the congregation of the Lord; even to his tenth generation shall he not enter into the congregation of the Lord."

I remember Dad saying Jesus was prejudiced and God was prejudiced, but really didn't believe it until I read the entire Bible. The Bible is filled with prejudicial statements about women, foreigners, non-Jews, rich people, and people with disabilities.

One of the most surprising parts of the Bible involves a directive from Jesus that was referenced earlier, but bears repeating. We all are aware of the controversy over prayers in our government buildings, including schools. The vitriolic commentary includes statements implying that if we reverted to earlier times, when everyone prayed all the time, the world would be a better place. If only the teachers and students could pray in schools (they actually can) the schools would not have such behavioral problems. However, in Chapter 6 of Matthew, Jesus himself teaches:

Matthew 6:5 - And when thou prayest, thou shalt not be as the hypocrites are: for they love to pray standing in the synagogues and in the corners of the streets, that they may be seen of men. Verily I say unto you, They have their reward.

Matthew 6:6 - But thou, when thou prayest, enter into thy closet, and when thou hast shut thy door, pray to thy Father which is in secret; and thy Father which seeth in secret shall reward thee openly.

It seems that the people who are so vehemently advocating for public prayer are disobeying the teachings of Jesus.

Curses/Destruction

◇◇

THE BIBLE SOMETIMES READS like a Stephen King novel, with the Lord imposing all kinds of mayhem, destruction, and plagues on people who have turned against him. Everyone knows about the flood that killed everyone except Noah and his family, but there are numerous other accounts of God either directly killing someone or directing others to kill them. He warns that people will eat their own sons and daughters (Leviticus 26:29), will be killed by plagues (Numbers 11:33; Zachariah 14:12), filled with worms (Act 12:23) and covered with boils from head to foot (Deuteronomy 28:59). God is rejoicing in his destruction (Deuteronomy 28:63) and, as mentioned before, is quite perverse in some of the punishments. People have to drink their own urine and eat their own excrement (2 Kings 18:27), and have their bowels rot away (2 Chronicles 21:15). Children are dashed on the pavement and women are raped (Isaiah 13:16) for rebelling against God.

While I was reading this, I couldn't help but notice the negative verses seemingly outnumbered the verses that spoke of God's love, which appear to be minimized in the horrid descriptions of destruction and anger. There are those who believe that God still uses his destructive powers to target certain groups. Chapters 36 and 37 of Job reveal that God controls weather, storms, etc. Some of the more evangelical persuasion still believe that hurricanes, tornadoes, landslides, tidal waves, and earthquakes are punishment from God.

Life and celebrations, according to the Bible, are worse than death. So, why are the evangelicals considered such pro-lifers? Ecclesiastes 4:3 tells us it is better not to be born, and Ecclesiastes 7: 1-2 says: "A good name is better than precious ointment; and the day of death than the day of one's birth. It is better to go to the house of mourning, than to go to the house of feasting; for that is the end of all men; and the living will lay it to his heart."

No wonder I hate weddings more than funerals. But, I thought it was the "in-your-face" sexism of weddings. Instead, it just happens to be biblically mandated. Who knew?

Beliefs are important, and do guide us in many of the decisions we adopt. If you steadfastly hold the belief that God determines whether we live or die and He or She determines the precise moment death will occur, you would probably be adamantly opposed to euthanasia. (I still have difficulty reconciling the ease with which the people who hold these beliefs take medication and agree to aggressive therapies to prolong their lives.) Those who do not believe that God makes those determinations would be much more likely, I suppose, to consider euthanasia as a viable alternative to the tremendous suffering from a terminal illness.

Religious beliefs, in many people's eyes also define our character. Religious beliefs in our political leaders are important because people equate those who are religious with positive characteristics, such as honesty and integrity. People who are religious are often perceived as more trustworthy, although there are numerous examples of religious leaders killing, committing adultery, molesting children, and embezzling church funds.

People who firmly hold that the Bible is the infallible word of God really need to understand its contents. Even Jimmy Carter, as cited in www.brainyquote.com, said, "I am a nuclear physicist by training and a deeply committed Christian. I don't have any doubt in my mind about God who created the entire universe. But, I don't adhere to passages that so and so was created 4000 years before Christ, and things of that kind." There, however, seems to be a real "disconnect" between biblical interpretations and science. Contrary to my father's beliefs, geologists and biologists **can** actually tell how old things are.

My purpose for trying to write the book was to try to encourage everyone to learn for themselves and think for themselves; to avoid being blindly led by Biblical "experts" who may be selective in the information that is shared. Of course, I was selective in the verses I chose to include; but do have admiration for those who choose to focus on the positive, uplifting teachings and philosophy of the Bible.

I do, however, think another Enlightenment period would serve us well and is needed. Reasonable dialogue about biblical teachings should not shake the faith of the committed Christians, yet non-believers have a difficult time taking seriously those who blindly proclaim that they believe the Bible is God's holy word when they do not have a full understanding of its contents. Perhaps the most disturbing is how many "believers" are so critical of others' religions. As is illustrated in the Bible, and continues in our contemporary lives, the belief that one religion is the only way to salvation has been the motivation for wars and mass murders, etc. We really do need to be saved from religion.

Should the United States adopt a Christian ruled government? I think any mandated religious government – Christian, Muslim, Judaism, and any others that are based on teachings that are thousands of years old, would be dangerous. Could you imagine if our citizens were suddenly forced to adhere to the teachings in the Bible? God help us all!

Depression

◇◇◇◇◇◇◇◇◇◇◇◇◇◇◇◇◇◇◇◇◇◇◇◇◇◇◇◇◇◇◇◇◇◇◇◇

MORE PEOPLE THAN EVER are diagnosed with depression. We have it better, in many respects, than any other generation, but more of us are depressed. Could it be that our ancestors did not have time to be depressed, because they were always working hard – sometimes motivated to build a better life for their families – so we, their children, and grand-children, would not have to work so hard?

So, why are there more and more depressed people? Could hard work be an absolute antidote, or prophylactically inhibit depressive tendencies, even in those who may have a genetic predisposition towards depression? This theory implies that we just need to return to an old-fashioned work ethic to prevent depressive episodes. Could it be that our tendency to be sedentary has contributed? Everyone knows that exercise is the best thing we can do to prevent depression – that we need fresh air and sunshine, and social support groups (that used to be called friends). But no one has really identified the specific reasons our society is more depressed.

One theory is that our 24/7 "wired" technology allows no mental breaks that are necessary for mental health. Anyone who watches the news all day cannot escape the stress that is encouraged by the media. Reporters tease, "Will North Korea fire nuclear weapons on the United States?" "Will our health insurance rise so much that nobody will be able to afford the premiums?" "Will gas prices skyrocket?" "Is a giant asteroid hurling towards the earth?" Stay tuned at 11:00.

Adulthood

I love being an adult – free from the constraints and restraints of parental authority and influence. My worst nightmares as an adult involve scenes where I am once again under the power of my parents, and once again dependent on their permission to go anywhere or do anything. In my nightmares, I only feel frustration and anger when I dream I am living under their command. This should not be.

I love making my own decisions, not being subjected to their criticism and derision for expressing thoughts that are different from their ingrained beliefs. I love being able to - with the constraints of being a responsible adult, of course – go where I want, when I want with whomever I choose; eat what I want, buy what I want, dance if I want to, drink a glass of wine with dinner; begin eating without having a lengthy blessing before every blasted meal, and not having to listen to that shrill, deafening tea kettle every morning signaling that the water is boiling.

FINAL THOUGHTS

◇◇

SINCE *EVANGELICAL* IS INCLUDED in the title of this book, I wanted to make sure I did not misrepresent my parents by calling them evangelical. So, I did some research and found that 36 percent of Americans surveyed by Ellison Research in 2008 had no idea what the word *evangelical* means. According to www.creationtips.com/evangelical.html, the National Association of Evangelicals defines an evangelical as someone who:

- believes that the Bible is authoritative
- has had a born-again experience
- shares this message of faith.

Oh, no – no misrepresentation here. My parents definitely fall into that category.

Despite their faults, and we all have them, my family has enormous strengths that helped contribute to positive outcomes for all of us. I realize I have been quite critical of my family, but understand that recognition of strengths is equally important. One of the things I appreciate most is that my mother, in particular, valued education, and pushed us to excel academically. The question for us was not, "Are you going to college?" The question was, "Which college are you going to attend?" She understood the value of self-sufficiency and wanted to make sure we were able to take care of ourselves. I cannot emphasize how grateful I am to my parents for providing me with an undergraduate degree (no student loan incurred) and a Master's degree.

While I was in high school and college, I worked a couple of years in tobacco. That experience was enough to motivate me to study hard and get a degree so I would not have to do that kind of work the rest of my life. Every time I didn't feel like studying, but knew I should, I thought of being on that harvester in the middle of a stinking tobacco field in the heat of the day in humid North Carolina, and I easily coerced myself into hitting the books.

I also appreciate my family's love of laughter and sense of humor. Even though I did not think the jokes were always appropriate, they understood that laughter was "good medicine for the soul." My older sister was nicknamed "Lucy" for her ability to keep us all in stitches. She was, indeed, a clown and loved to make people laugh. Our house was filled with laughter much of the time. My sister also possesses an amazing capacity to forgive, as she has demonstrated numerous times. She loves her grandchildren more than I thought anyone was capable of loving anything.

My younger sister, when we were growing up, was the sweetest, most gentle, compassionate, tender-hearted soul in existence. She has hardened some, thank goodness, because she would never be a successful teacher without a tough skin. But, underneath that tough exterior she has formed, we realize that she continues to be a loving, compassionate soul who is enormous fun to be around.

She is also a great golfer. Golfers will appreciate that she, who didn't begin playing golf until she was an adult, has made two holes in one – much to the chagrin of her husband who taught her to play and has not managed one hole in one. Her compact frame is as powerful as her personality. She and her husband enjoy life and continue to play and travel whenever they can. She is the most patient and gentle of us in her dealings with our father.

Mother surprised us all late in her life. We were playing a game that describes how one thinks and feels about certain topics. Mother said she would like to be a stand-up comedian. We should have guessed when she seemed to enjoy her performance as a crazy person at a church camp. At the Free Will Baptist Camp, Cragmont, in Black Mountain, North Carolina, we always had a talent show the night before the camp session ended and we headed for home. This talent show was taken very seriously, and the performers would practice for hours for their chance to shine in this safe setting as we all sat around the bonfire in the crisp, mountain air. I had no idea my mother was going to perform, but she sang "They're Coming to Take me Away" and was quite convincing as a person desperately in need of immediate hospitalization. "They're coming to take me away, ho, ho – to the funny farm where life is beautiful all the time, and I'll be happy to see those nice young men in their clean white coats, and they're coming to take me away, ha, ha." Mother would sometimes use humor to get us out of bed in the morning, and motivate us to complete our chores. There was nothing better than a family dinner when everyone was in a good mood, there was no "spilled milk" and mother would laugh uncontrollably at something someone else said or did. She had such a musical, contagious laughter.

We were hugged almost as much as we were hit, and I feel confident we were praised almost as much as we were criticized. I realize that we were so lucky in most respects. We never even came close to being sexually abused, except for that one uncle whose hand seemed to stray a little when we hugged him; and we never feared that our parents would split. So we were fortunate indeed to have such a stable, nurturing family. Although we were not wealthy by any means, and could not afford some of the luxuries our friends and neighbors enjoyed, we never went to bed hungry, even though we ate plenty of chicken pot pies. I think they cost 29 cents each at the time. Mother recalled the times when she was growing up when her ten siblings and she would get nothing but cornbread and milk for dinner. Sometimes, she had that herself – perhaps to bring back memories of those special times. We never lacked for nice clothes, even though I wore hand-me-downs from my older sister. As a dyke, however, I would have much rather wear hand-me-downs than go shopping for new clothes.

My parents had to be very thrifty, but they could really stretch a dollar. My father's passion seemed to be to find a good sale, so I don't think he ever paid full price for anything that could potentially be put on sale. As a result, we received good quality clothing at a great price.

Our basic needs were more than met. We did not have to worry, as some children do, that our parents would come home drunk or stoned out of their minds, and become unpredictably abusive. We did not have to worry that they would have a big argument and someone would leave. We did not have to worry that they would divorce. Despite all their faults, we were fortunate to have a family who had such strong principles and were truly interested in helping to create a better place for us. To everyone who has played a role in my upbringing, I would like to express my sincere gratitude. The product is far from perfect, but the journey has been truly fascinating.

ABOUT THE AUTHOR

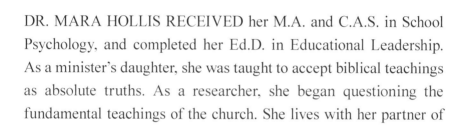

DR. MARA HOLLIS RECEIVED her M.A. and C.A.S. in School Psychology, and completed her Ed.D. in Educational Leadership. As a minister's daughter, she was taught to accept biblical teachings as absolute truths. As a researcher, she began questioning the fundamental teachings of the church. She lives with her partner of 29 years in North Carolina.